The Arbitration Series – Volume 1

HARMONY *amidst* DISHARMONY

The Indian Framework

A commentary on
India's arbitration law
since August 1996.
It's 'a whole new ball game'.

By the Same Author

India's Legal System: Can It Be Saved? (2006)

Before Memory Fades: An Autobiography (2010)

The State of the Nation (2013)

God Save the Hon'ble Supreme Court (2018)

Harmony amidst Disharmony: The International Framework (The Arbitration Series—Volume 2) (2020)

You Must Know Your Constitution (2023)

Beyond the Courtroom (2025)

Legally Speaking (2025)

The Arbitration Series – Volume 1

HARMONY *amidst* DISHARMONY

The Indian Framework

FALI S. NARIMAN

HAY HOUSE

HAY HOUSE INDIA

New Delhi • London • Sydney
Carlsbad, California • New York City

Hay House Publishers (India) Pvt Ltd
Muskaan Complex, Plot No. 3, B-2, Vasant Kunj, New Delhi – 110 070, India

Hay House LLC, P.O. Box 5100, Carlsbad, CA 92018-5100, USA
Hay House UK Ltd, 1st Floor, Crawford Corner, 91-93 Baker Street, London W1U 6QQ, UK
Hay House Australia Publishing Pty Ltd, 18/36 Ralph St., Alexandria NSW 2015, Australia

Email: contact@hayhouse.co.in
Website: www.hayhouse.co.in

First published by Hay House India in Hardcover, 2020
Paperback edition, 2022
Reprint, 2026
16 15 14 13 12 11 10 9 8 7

ISBN 978-93-91067-46-5

Printed at Repro India Limited

MIX
Paper from responsible sources
FSC® C047271
FSC www.fsc.org

Hay House is committed to a sustainable future for our business, our readers and our planet. This book is made from Forest Stewardship Council® certified paper.

To

The memory of Dr P. Chandrasekhara Rao (22 April 1936—11 October 2018), the draftsman, who inspired and contributed much to what was then an entirely new law of arbitration for India—The Arbitration and Conciliation Act, 1996—as was enacted. His contribution was invaluable and will be long remembered.

Contents

1

The Beginning

Arbitration in British India

Ancient India had an indigenous tradition of resolving disputes between individuals or groups of people. Affairs of the community were managed by a headman or a village council of five or more members—'Panchas' or 'Panchayat'.[1] The sanction against the disobedience of its decisions was exclusion from all religious and social functions of the community, and at times, even excommunication.

During the British period, from the year 1600, the East India Company was incorporated by Royal Charter (by Queen Elizabeth-I), and was first established in Bengal (now West Bengal) and Benaras (now Varanasi); Regulations[2] were framed by the Company in exercise of powers granted to it by England's Parliament. The Bengal Regulations (of 1772 and 1781) had provided that parties to a dispute relating to accounts "shall submit the dispute to arbitration", but arbitration was recognised only in suits (or actions) filed in court.

The muffassal courts (i.e. the courts in the districts) were established (in British India) by the East India Company from the year 1773: to administer for the "Hindoos" the "Hindoo" laws (before they were codified), and for the "Mohammedans" the "Mohammedan"[3] law in family matters and matters of succession to property[4].

***

The British governance of India[5] effectively began in 1786 with Lord Cornwallis being appointed Governor-General of India and Commander-in-Chief. Lord Cornwallis, (as Governor-General), gave effect to directions received from the Board of Commissioners for Indian Affairs established by Parliament in England[6], and framed rules for the administration of justice founded on the ancient law and local usages prevailing in various parts of India.

It was during this time that regulations relating to arbitration were framed[7] for arbitration in suits filed in courts.

The Legislative Council for India was established in the year 1834 and the first enactment to regulate civil courts was under Act VIII of 1859—known as the Code of Civil Procedure Act, 1859: (C.P.C. of 1859). It codified the Civil Procedure in civil courts and provided inter alia for reference to arbitration between parties to suits filed in the courts. It also permitted (for the first time) references of disputes to arbitration by parties in civil suits without the intervention of the court.

The Code of Civil Procedure of 1859, introduced:

- Sections 312 to 325 (dealing with arbitration between parties to a suit);
- Section 326 (dealing with filing in court of an agreement between two or more parties to refer existing disputes and differences to arbitration without the intervention of the court); and
- Section 327 (providing for the filing in court by the arbitrator of his award).

The provisions of the Code of Civil Procedure, 1859 were re-enacted, with modifications, by laws subsequently enacted viz. by Act X of 1877—C.P.C. of 1877; then, by Act XIV of 1882—C.P.C. of 1882, and ultimately by Act V of 1908. The Civil Procedure Code 1908 (C.P.C. 1908) with subsequent amendments remains in operation today[8].

Each of these codes (of Civil Procedure) recognised references to arbitration but only of disputes which had actually arisen (not future disputes), and also provided for reference of such disputes to an arbitrator named by the parties. In the eighteenth century, courts of justice had been set up for the three presidency towns of Calcutta, Madras and Bombay (now Kolkata, Chennai and Mumbai, respectively), conferring on them jurisdiction to administer—within the presidency towns— English Common Law (as well as English statutes) "so far as could be made applicable under circumstances prevailing in India."[9] Ultimately in each of the three presidency towns, high courts were established in the year 1862, with the issue of Letters Patents by Royal Command.

Ten years later, the Indian Contract Act, 1872 was enacted by the Indian legislature: and in tune with the English law of that period, contracts that ousted the jurisdiction of courts in India were declared void, with a saving clause (enacted only by way of an exception) in respect of contracts referring to arbitration "any dispute which may arise" between the parties to the contract" (Section 28).

"Section 28: (Agreements in restraint of legal proceedings void") had affirmed the common-law-rule initially recognised by English courts prohibiting all agreements ousting the jurisdiction of courts. In the current predilection around the world with a whole range of *alternative* methods of dispute—resolution with particular emphasis on conciliation and mediated settlements—including India joining the latest: the "Singapore Convention"[10] (UN Convention on International Settlement Agreements resulting from Mediation)—which opened for signature by all states on and from 1 August 2019—the continuance in operation of Section 28 of the 1872 Act remains an inexplicable anachronism.

Since there was no provision made for a reference to arbitration of *future* disputes, the first substantive law (enacted mainly for that purpose) was the Indian Arbitration Act (IX of 1899)—which was based on the provisions of England's Arbitration Act of 1899. It made provision for reference of present as well as future disputes, to arbitration without the intervention of the court.[11] However, the provisions of the (Indian) Arbitration Act, 1899 of 1[11]899 were applicable only to "Presidency" towns[12] (i.e. to Bombay, Madras, and Calcutta). It did not apply to the rest of British India).

From 1899 onwards, arbitration became (to a limited extent), a mechanism to resolve disputes (including disputes of a commercial nature) outside the court system, but the enforcement and the setting aside of an arbitral award remained with the courts. When arbitrators did not follow the law, their awards were nullified by the courts. Keeping in mind the provision contained in Section 28 of the Contract Act, 1872, the Privy Council held—in *Champsey Bhara* vs. *Jivraj Balloo Spinning and Weaving Co. Ltd.* (1923)[13]—that an award could be set aside if (in the opinion of the court) there was an error of law on the face of the award, which went to the root of the matter and vitiated the award as a whole.

***

During the British period in India (after the First World War) the Geneva Protocol (of 1923) and thereafter the Geneva Convention for the Execution of Arbitral Awards (of 1927) were promulgated by the League of Nations at the instance of the then newly formed International Chamber of Commerce (ICC) in Paris. The Protocol and the Convention were acceded to not only by the United Kingdom but also by its colonies including British India. The Arbitration (Protocol and Convention) Act, 1937 (the 1937 Act) was then enacted in British India in recognition of, and in implementation of, British India's acceptance of the Geneva Protocol of 1923 and the Geneva Convention of 1927. One of the main provisions of the 1937 Act was Section 3 which stated that a court *shall* make an order staying all proceedings in a suit in respect of contracts containing an arbitration clause:

> . . . Unless (the court was) satisfied that the agreement for arbitration has become inoperative or cannot proceed, or that there is not in fact any dispute between the parties with regard to the matter agreed to be referred . . .[14]

Reported judgments of High Courts in India on the provisions of the 1937 Act (especially Section 3) are mentioned in the endnote.[15]

Meanwhile, in the year 1938, the Government of India examined the question of amending the law of arbitration in the entire country; and after taking into consideration the provisions of the English Arbitration Act, of 1934[16] the Indian Arbitration Act of 1940 was enacted. It contained, for the first time, a comprehensive law of arbitration which applied throughout India. Although England's Parliament kept updating its arbitration law by enacting Arbitration Acts of 1950, 1975, 1979 (and ultimately, the Arbitration Act of 1996), India's substantive law of arbitration remained as provided for in the 1940 Act. Decades later, it got replaced and repealed by the Arbitration and Conciliation Act, 1996—since updated by two amendments:

(i) by the Arbitration and Conciliation (Amendment) Act 2015 (Act 3 of 2016); and

(ii) by the Arbitration and Conciliation Amendment Act No. 33 of 2019.

The Arbitration Act, 1940 (10 of 1940)[17]—was an Act to consolidate and amend the law relating to arbitration. It applied throughout India. It consisted of seven chapters:

Chapter I—Introductory including definitions
Chapter II—Arbitration without the intervention of the court (Sections 3-19) including Section 17 (Judgment to be passed in terms of award)
Chapter III—Arbitration with the intervention of the court where there is no suit pending): Section 20
Chapter IV—Arbitration in suits: Sections 21 to 25
Chapter V—General: (Sections 26 to 38), including:

Section 30 (conferring power on courts to set aside or remit awards);[18]
Section 32 (bar of suits on arbitration agreements as well as on awards);
Section 33 (application for a declaration that an arbitration agreement exists);[19] and
Section 34 (Power to stay legal proceedings where there is an arbitration agreement) that empowered (but did not compel) the court in which a suit was filed to enforce the provisions of the contract to stay the suit where the contract contained an agreement to refer disputes to arbitration between parties to the suit.

Chapter VI—Appeals (Section 39)
Chapter VII—Miscellaneous: (Sections 40-49 and including Sections 46 and 47[20])

After the enactment of the Arbitration Act, 1940, decisions of the Supreme Court of India, along the lines of the opinion of the Privy Council in *Champsey Bhara* (1923), (already quoted) were the following: in *Alopi Pershad* vs. *Union of India* AIR 1960 S.C. 588; *Union of India* vs. *Rallia Ram* AIR 1963 S.C. 1685; Coimbatore *DPT Sangam* vs. *B. S. Foundry* 1987 (3) SCC 723.[21]

The old English case of *Hodgkinson* vs. *Fernie* (1857), reported in 140 English Reports 712—first referred to by the Privy Council in *Champsey Bhara* (1923)—was followed in India; for instance, in *UOI* vs. *Bungo Steel* AIR 1967 S.C. 103; in *Raipur Development* vs. *Chokhamal Contractors* 1989 (2) SCC 721, 732; in *Trustees of the Port of Madras* vs. *Engineering Constructions* 1995 (5) SCC

531, 538; in *Bhagwati Oxygen Ltd.* vs. *Hindustan Copper Ltd.* 2005 (6) SCC 462 at 473; and in *Associate Builders* vs. *Delhi Development Authority* (DDA) 2015 (3) SCC 49 at pages 79 and 80.

All these cases, though reported after the enactment of the Arbitration and Conciliation Act, 1996, (which came into force in August 1996), were decisions rendered under the Arbitration Act, 1940, (which had stood repealed by the 1996 Act).

Error-of-Law jurisdiction, though abolished by the English Arbitration Act, 1979 [Section 1(1) and (4) replacing Section 21 of the English Arbitration Act, 1950]—continued to apply in India under the 1940 Act: e.g. in *Indu Engineering and Textiles Ltd.* vs. *Delhi Development Authority* AIR 2001 S.C. 2668 at 2670-2671; quoting *Halsbury's Laws of England* Vol.-2 (4th Ed.) para 624; in *Amravati District Central Co-operative* vs. *United Indian Fire and General Insurance* 2010 (5) SCC 294 at 305; in *Sharma and Associates Contractors Pvt. Ltd.* vs. *Progressive Constructions Ltd.* 2017 (5) SCC 743 para 12 and 13[22]. All these cases, although decided, and reported, after the coming into force of the 1996 Act were cases that had arisen and were decided under the Arbitration Act, 1940 (which had stood repealed by the 1996 Act).

***

The Geneva Convention of 1927, was superseded by the much more comprehensive (and far more successful) New York Convention on the Recognition and Enforcement of Foreign Awards 1958.[23] It made provision not only for recognition of arbitration agreements for reference to arbitration anywhere other than in the contracting state, but also provided for recognition and enforcement (in the contracting state) of arbitral awards made outside the contracting state ("foreign awards"). The Republic of India was one of the original signatories to the New York Convention 1958, and on its ratification by the Government of India on 13 July 1960, India's Parliament enacted the first implementing law viz. the Foreign Awards (Recognition and Enforcement) Act, 1961[24] (in supersession of the 1937 Act).

But, the 1961 Act was not just a non-starter, it was also a failure. Section 3 of the Act ("stay of proceedings in respect of matters to be referred to arbitration"), though in the same mandatory terms as Section 3 of the Arbitration Protocol and Convention Act of 1937, failed to conform to the language adopted in Article II(3) of the New York Convention. And when this was pointed out by India's Supreme Court in *Tractoroexport Moscow* vs. *M/s Tarapore & Co* AIR 1971 S.C. page 1, some years later the 1961 Act was amended by Amending Act 47 of 1973. The Indian Parliament, only then, altered the language of Section 3 of the 1961 Act, to make it conform to Article II(3) of the Convention. In *National Thermal Power Corporation* vs. *Singer* AIR 1993 SC 998, a decision by a Bench of two judges of India's Supreme Court, it was held (wrongly interpreting the provisions of Section 9 of the 1961 Act)[25] that when an award had been made under an arbitration agreement "governed by the law of India" the award—even if rendered outside India—was to be treated as a domestic award and could be set aside under India's Arbitration Act, 1940. The decision of the court in *National Thermal Power Corporation* was per incuriam: and had been characterized by Gary Born, in his two-volume tome (of over four thousand pages) titled *International Commercial Arbitration* (2nd Edition) as an "idiosyncratic" decision!

Until the enactment of the Arbitration Act, 1940 the common law right to file a suit in India to enforce an arbitral award had been recognised.

For example, in the early 1920s, a suit was filed in the High Court of Madras against a defendant (a resident of Madras) for a decree to be passed against the defendant (on an award made in London) for sums payable under an arbitral award made in London. A single judge (Justice Coutts Trotter) of the High Court of Madras—a chartered high court governed by its Letters Patent —assumed jurisdiction and entertained the suit, passing a decree in terms of the London Award. His decision was upheld by the Privy Council (then the last Court of Appeal from judgments of courts in India)—reversing a Division Bench judgment of the High Court of Madras. The case: *L. Oppenheim & Co.* vs. *Haji Mohamed Haneef* is reported in AIR 1920 Privy Council, page 120 as well as in 1922 (1) Appeal Cases 482 P.C.[26] It is a case mentioned in almost all books on arbitration law.[27]

In the year 1927, a Full Bench decision of the Bombay High Court—(a Bench presided over by its Chief Justice, Sir Amberson Marten)—held that, the common law of England applied to arbitrations in India.[28] Later, in the year 1934, the Bombay High Court (in *Mathuradas* vs. *Maganlal)*, observed that the law of arbitration, as then enacted (i.e. the Act of 1899), was not exhaustive, and that the common law right to refer, to arbitration by oral agreement, was in existence in India and was not abrogated at the date when the Indian Arbitration Act, 1899 was passed. It held that the common law right was not taken away by the Arbitration Act 1899, since a party could file a suit on the award which right was given under the common law and not by statute[29]. However, all this changed after the enactment of India's Arbitration Act 1940, which included Section 32: ("Bar to suit contesting arbitration agreement or awards") and so long as the 1940 Act remained in force—till October 1996 (which was the date of coming into force of the 1996 Act)—the civil remedy of a suit on an award was barred[30].

In the United Kingdom, an arbitral award could always be enforced under the Common Law by bringing an "action on the award", even after the enactment of England's Arbitration Act 1996[31]: the reason being that the claim on the award is a claim arising out of a breach of an implied obligation to fulfil any resulting arbitral award. However, the claimant had to show that the award was valid and final according to the law governing the arbitral proceedings. This enforcement under the Common Law continues to be available in England in respect of all types of arbitral awards, whether foreign or domestic.

***

Between the year 1937 (India's first enactment implementing British India's accession to the Geneva Convention on Execution of Awards, 1927) and October 1996 (date of commencement of India's Arbitration and

Conciliation Act, 1996), there were three separate laws dealing with arbitration in India:

[i] The Arbitration (Protocol and Convention) Act, 1937 implementing British India's accession to the Geneva Convention of 1927 on the Execution of (Foreign) Awards;

[ii] The Arbitration Act, 1940—(which repealed the Arbitration Act of 1899)—a consolidated law of arbitration dealing almost entirely with domestic arbitration (except for sections 46 and 47); and

[iii] The Foreign Awards (Recognition and Enforcement) Act, 1961—the first enactment of the Republic of India implementing India's ratification of the New York Convention on the Recognition and Enforcement (*of Arbitration Agreements*[32]) and of Foreign Awards 1958 (in supersession of the Geneva Convention on Execution of Arbitration Awards 1927)[33].

With the simultaneous existence of the three separate laws[34] court decisions on international commercial arbitration (prior to the 1996 Act) were neither uniform nor consistent as illustrated by the following binding decisions of the Supreme Court of India:

- In 1959, the Supreme Court of India held in *Shiva Jute Baling Ltd.* vs. *Hindley and Co.*[35] that where a contract provided for arbitration in accordance with the bye-laws of the London Jute Association and also provided that courts of England will have exclusive jurisdiction over all disputes which might arise thereunder ("except for the purpose of enforcing in the colonies abroad any arbitration award made under the contract"); and since an award was obtained from the London Jute Association in October 1949, by Hindley and Company Ltd. and the company had then filed the foreign award in the High Court of Calcutta and prayed that judgment be pronounced in accordance with the award (under section 17 of the Arbitration Act of 1940) and a decree be passed; when the same was resisted, both a single judge as well as a Division Bench of the Calcutta High Court[36] *held that the award was not contrary to the law of India and was capable of being enforced in India; a view that was later affirmed by the Supreme Court of India;*[37].

- In 1963, in *Michael Goldodetz* vs. *Serajjuddin, AIR 1963 SC 1044*, (a case under Arbitration [Protocol and Convention] Act, 1937) a bench of four judges of the Supreme Court of India reversed the decision of a Division Bench of two judges of the Calcutta High Court (reported in AIR 1960 Cal. 46) holding that an arbitration clause in the contract providing for arbitration in New York did not preclude the Calcutta High Court from entertaining a suit at the instance of the Indian party to the contract, and also did not preclude a single judge of the Calcutta High Court from exercising his discretion under Section 34 of the Arbitration Act, 1940 (as he had done in the case) not to stay that suit on grounds of convenience, equity and justice;

- In 1964, in *Societe De Traction Evapo Transporation* vs. *Kamani Engineering Corporation (reported in AIR 1964 S.C. 558)*, a suit had been filed in the High Court of Bombay by an Indian party in respect of a collaboration agreement with a French Company. It contained an arbitration clause for resolution of disputes by arbitration in accordance with the rules of the International Chamber of Commerce (ICC) Court of International Arbitration Paris. A motion was filed by the French company to stay the suit in Bombay. A Division Bench of the high court (unreported) refused to stay the suit (because of certain mandatory provisions of Indian Company Law). The Supreme Court of India set aside the decision of the Division Bench of the Bombay High Court and held that an agreement between the parties to refer all disputes to arbitration according to the ICC rules was binding on the Indian company, and since the Indian company had filed a suit against the foreign company in a court in India on the basis of a Collaboration Agreement, then under Section 3 of the Arbitration (Protocol and Convention) Act, 1937 (implementing the Geneva Convention of 1927) the suit had to be stayed. For reaching this conclusion the Supreme Court of India relied on the provisions of Section 47 of the Arbitration Act, 1940 ("Act to apply to all Arbitrations");

  * Also in the year 1964, in *Badat and Co.* vs. *East India Trading Co.*, AIR 1964 SC 538 (a Bench of 3 judges)—(in a case under the Arbitration Protocol

and Convention Act, 1937)—it was held by the Supreme Court of India that, foreign awards and foreign judgments based on those awards were enforceable on the same grounds and in the same circumstances in which they were enforceable in England, under the Common Law of England, on grounds of justice, equity and good conscience. In that case the suit in Bombay based on the foreign award (made in New York) was however dismissed (by the Supreme Court) by majority 2:1—the presiding judge on the Bench of 3 judges dissenting, because according to the majority (2 out of 3 judges) the award in New York under the New York law did not become final until judgment was given upon the award; (and since judgment on the New York Award had been in fact given), the award by itself furnished no cause of action for a suit filed in India on the award; only the judgment obtained in New York would furnish a cause of action; a suit on the foreign judgment would have been then maintainable (under Section 13 of the CPC 1908). It was held by the two judges (majority) that although the High Court of Bombay had jurisdiction to enforce a final award made in foreign arbitration, in the particular case the award not being final, it did not furnish a valid cause of action for the suit;[38]

* In 1985, in *Renusagar Power Co. Ltd.* vs. General Electric Company and Another (Renusagar–I)—a case under the Foreign Awards Recognition and Enforcement Act 1961, reported in AIR 1985 SC 1156, emphasis

was rightly laid on the mandatory "shall" (in reference to foreign arbitrations held abroad) in contrast with the discretionary "may" in Section 34 of the Arbitration Act, 1940 (in the case of domestic arbitration);

- In 1987, in *ONGC* (Indian Company) vs. *Western Company of North America* (US Company) AIR 1987 SC 674, a drilling contract containing an arbitration clause provided that arbitration proceedings shall be held in accordance with the Arbitration Act, 1940 and the interpretation of the contract was to be governed by the laws of India. An award having been made by the umpire under the Arbitration Act, 1940[39], the US Company instituted an action (suit) in a US court for a judgment in terms of the umpire's award, the award having been made by the umpire *in London*. It was held by the Supreme Court of India that because of Section 17 of the Arbitration Act, 1940, (judgment to be passed in terms of the award) an award under the Arbitration Act 1940 was "lifeless" and could not be enforced until it was made a rule of the court; it was consequently held that the High Court of Bombay had therefore power to grant an injunction restraining the American Company from proceeding further with its application in the US Court for a decree on the award. The Supreme Court of India upheld the restraining order passed by the High Court of Bombay—but in the peculiar facts of the case imposed certain additional terms and conditions on the Indian company;

- In 1993 (in yet another case, already referred to, also under the Foreign Awards Recognition and Enforcement Act, 1961) *NTPC* vs. *Singer Corporation* AIR 1993 S.C. 998, NTPC being an Indian Company, and Singer Corporation being a US Company, an award was made in London. It was sought to be set aside in India by an application filed in the Delhi High Court under Section 30 of the Arbitration Act, 1940[40] then in force. A Division Bench of the Delhi High Court in a judgment reported in [1991(1) Arb. L. R. 313 (Delhi)], (rightly) rejected the application as not maintainable, but the Supreme Court of India set aside the Delhi High Court judgment holding that the Foreign Awards (Recognition and Enforcement) Act, 1961 did not apply because of the saving clause (Section 9 (b) of the Act): it read: "nothing in the Act shall apply to any award made on an arbitration agreement governed by the law of India". The case was remanded back to the Delhi High Court to decide the application for setting aside the London award on merits. The view taken in *NTPC* vs. *Singer* (by a Bench of two judges of the Supreme Court), was re-asserted by a bench decision of three judges (of the Supreme Court) in *Sumitomo Heavy Industries* vs. *Oil and Natural Gas Commission* AIR 1998 SC 825 a case under the 1961 Act and also in connection with a London Award.[41]

- In 1994, *in Svenska Handelsbanken* vs. *Indian Charge Chrome Ltd.* (1994) 2 SCC 155, (a case under the 1961 Act) it was held by India's Supreme Court overruling a decision (of June 1993) of the High Court of Orissa, that parties having agreed to arbitration were not precluded from filing a suit in court, but an application under Section 3 of the Foreign Awards (Recognition and Enforcement) Act, 1961 would lie for stay of the suit. It was held that *right to a foreign arbitration was an indefeasible right in which the court did not have any discretion.* But it was also held that since the requirements of Section 3 of the Foreign Awards (Recognition and Enforcement) Act, 1961 had been satisfied, a suit by the Indian party could be filed in India; but when filed it had to be stayed, under the Foreign Awards Recognition and Enforcement Act, 1961 (to enable arbitration of the dispute to go on in Stockholm according to Swedish law).

End Notes:

1. (Vytla) *Sitanna* vs. *Marivada Viranna and Others*, AIR 1934 P.C. 105, 107 (Sir John Wallis sitting in England's Privy Council in a case in appeal from the High Court of Madras mentioned the Panchayat system as "the time-honoured method of deciding disputes. . . "
2. "Regulation" was the limited power of legislation given to the Government of the Presidencies after the statutes enacted by the British Parliament. See M. P. Jain: *Outlines of Indian Legal History*, N. M. Tripathi Ltd., Bombay, 3rd Edition, 1972, p. 470.

3. This is how "Hindu" was then spelt by the British! The word "Mohammedan" was previously used to describe a follower of the Prophet. The words "Muslim" and "Islamic" are more common today.
4. See A Gledhill: *The Republic of India*, Greenwood Press, 1970, 1st Edition, p. 150.
5. British India then included the entire sub-continent: the territory of what is now the Republic of India (since 1950), as well as the territory which became (in 1950) the Islamic Republic of Pakistan which also included East Bengal, which later, (from 1972) became independent from Pakistan and proclaimed itself as the People's Republic of Bangladesh; Burma (now Myanmar) too was a part of British India, until it was separated in 1935 by Acts of Britain's Parliament.
6. The British Parliament had passed a statute in 1786 to establish a Board of Commissioners for Indian Affairs. See also Tagore Law Lectures—N. N. Sircar: *The Law of Arbitration in British India*, Calcutta University, Calcutta, 1942, Pp. 5-6.
7. The Bengal Regulations-I (of 1772, 1781, 1787)—made provisions for a settlement of parties' disputes; The Bengal Regulation XVI (of 1793)— prescribed rules for encouraging arbitration in suits before the Civil Court; The Bengal Regulations XV (of 1795 and 1803), and The Bengal Regulation VI (of 1813) prohibited vakils from being employed as arbitrators, but this was rescinded by Bengal Regulation XXVII (of 1814 [section 19]; The Bombay Regulation-I (of 1799); The Bombay Regulations—IV and VI (of 1827)—(were passed to facilitate in the Bombay Presidency the amicable adjustment of disputes of a civil nature by means of arbitrators); The Madras Regulations-I (of 1802) gave certain powers for calling in Panchayats for settling disputes; The Madras Regulations IV and V were passed to encourage awards by village Panchayats and

machinery was provided for working out the scheme with the help of village Munsiffs; but the village munsiff had no power to annul an award; By Madras Regulation—VII (of 1822)—Revenue matters were referred for arbitration and collectors were directed to encourage parties to refer disputes to arbitration.

8. Section 89 of the C.P.C. 1908, (as initially enacted), provided that the provisions relating to arbitration in the (prior) Code of Civil Procedure 1882 (namely Sections 506 to 526) would stand transferred to a Schedule—the Second Schedule to the C.P.C. 1908. Section 89(1) then read as follows:

   "Save in so far as otherwise provided by the Indian Arbitration Act, 1899, or by any other law for the time being in force, all references to arbitration whether by an order in a suit or otherwise, and all proceedings there under shall be governed by the provisions contained in the Second Schedule."

   This Section (along with the Second Schedule to the C.P.C. of 1908) was repealed by Section 49(1) of the British India's Arbitration Act of 1940—an amending and consolidating law with respect to arbitration.

9. In each of the three presidency-towns—Calcutta, Madras and Bombay— there were first established a Mayor's Court, then a Recorder's Court, and later, for, a brief period, a Supreme Court. They were replaced in 1862 by High Courts established by Royal Charter.

10. The text of the Singapore Convention is available at: https://www.uncitral.org/pdf/english/commissionsessions/51st-session/Annex_I.pdf

11. Under Section 2(a) of the Arbitration Act, 1899 "submission" meant a written agreement to submit present or future differences to arbitration, whether an arbitrator is named therein or not. This definition was repeated in

the Arbitration Act, 1940 under Section 2(a) "arbitration agreement".

12. In *Mathurdas* vs. *Maganlal,* ILR 58 Bom. 369 = AIR 1934 Bom 79 at 81, the High Court of Bombay held that the Act applied only to arbitrations which were connected either as to the subject matter, or as the parties, within the presidency towns.
13. In AIR 1923 P.C. 66 (an opinion of the Privy Council in a case from India) Lord Dunedin cited with approval a former decision of the British Court in *Hodgkinson* vs. *Fernie* Case (1857) 140 ER 712) that held that the arbitrator remains the sole and final judge on all questions of both of law and fact (with the only exception where the award is the result of corruption or fraud), and that where a question of law necessarily arose on the face of the award or upon some paper accompanying and forming part of the award and was wrongly decided, the court was empowered to set it aside.
14. Repealed by Section 85 of India's Arbitration and Conciliation Act 1996.
15. Viz.
    (i) *W. Wood & Sons Ltd.* vs. *Bengal Corporation & Anr.* reported in AIR 1956 Cal 238;
    (ii) *Mury Exportation* vs. *D. Khaitan & Sons Ltd.*, AIR 1956 Cal 644;
    (iii) *Bajrang Electric Steel Co. Private Ltd.* vs. *Commissioners for the Port of Calcutta and others,* AIR 1957 Cal 240;
    (iv) *S. Mohd. Naim Mohd. Alam* vs. *Rouraffic and Far Eastern Ltd.,* AIR 1960 Cal 146.
    (v) *Pratabmull Rameswar* vs. *K.C. Sethia* (*1944*) *Ltd.,* AIR 1960 Cal 702.
    (vi) *U.D. Patel and Co.* vs. *C. M. Milligam and Clarke Ltd.* AIR 1956 Bom 598;
    (vii) *M/s. Francesco Corsi* vs. *M/s. Gorakhram Golakchand,* AIR 1960 Bom 91; and

(viii) *Se Se Oil* vs. *Gorakhram Gokalchand*, 1962 (64) Bom L R 113.

16. Before the latest English Arbitration Act of 1996, in England (apart from its first Arbitration Law of 1899, the law of arbitration was contained in the Arbitration Acts of 1934, 1950 and 1979. These laws applied to different aspects of arbitration and was complemented by a large body of case-law. The latest English Arbitration Act of 1996 is to be construed in accordance with three guiding principles: fairness, party autonomy, and non-intervention by courts.
17. Repealed by the provisions of Section 85 of the 1996 Act.
18. Following decisions of courts in England and in India to set aside awards which disclosed on their face (or in a document annexed to the award) an error of law apparent on the face of the award, a single judge of the High Court of Bombay (Justice Variava), in the case of *National Housing Bank* vs. *ANZ Grindlays Bank PLC* (Judgment dt. 4 February 1998—(Reported in www.lawyerservices.in) or 1998 (2) LJ 153)—set aside an award (of an arbitral tribunal presided over by a retired chief justice of India), because on a question of law the award preferred to rely upon a decision of a Bench of 2 judges of the Supreme Court of India in preference to the decision of a Bench of 5 judges! This was presumably because under the Constitution of India (Article 141) it is expressly provided that the law declared by the Supreme Court is binding on all courts within the territory of India. On an appeal to the Supreme Court of India by ANZ Grindlays Bank the matter got settled without any opinion being expressed about the decision of Justice Variava (later, a Judge in the Supreme Court of India).
19. Section 32 and 33 of 1940 Act had been introduced at the suggestion of the Civil Justice Committee to negative the decision of the Privy Council in *R. D. Sasson* vs. *Ramdutt* 50 Cal 1 P.C: AIR 1922 P.C. page 374. When in a suit to set

aside an award it had been argued that the suit would not lie as the only remedy was to move the court to set aside the award under Section 14 of the Arbitration Act 1899 , the argument was rejected. It was observed: (at page 377):

> "Any objection to an award on the ground of misconduct or irregularity on the part of the arbitrator ought, no doubt, to be taken by motion to set aside the award; but where (as here) it is alleged that an arbitrator has acted wholly without jurisdiction, his award can be questioned in a suit brought for that purpose. Nor is the fact, that the award has been enforced by execution under Section 15, a bar to a suit to have it declared void and for consequential relief. Section 15 does not enact that the award, when filed, is to be deemed to be a decree of the Court, but only that it is to be enforceable as if it were a decree."

The purpose of Section 32 of the 1940 Act, was to establish only one court as the sole arbiter of all matters concerning arbitration: as was held in *Nathulal* vs. *Beharilal*: AIR 1952 Nagpur 65 at 67.

20. The Arbitration Act 1940 dealt with domestic arbitrations. However, Section 46 and Section 47 did provide as follows:

> "**46.** Application of Act to statutory arbitrations. The provisions of this Act, except sub-section (1) of section 6 and section 7, 12, 2 [,36] and 37, shall apply to every arbitration under any other enactment for the time being in force, as if the arbitration were pursuant to an arbitration agreement and as if that other enactment were an arbitration agreement, except in so far as this Act is inconsistent with that other enactment or with any rules made thereunder."
>
> "**47.** Act to apply to all arbitrations. Subject to the provisions of Section 46, and save in so far as is otherwise provided by any law for the time being in force, the

provisions of this Act shall apply to all arbitrations and to all proceedings thereunder: Provided that an arbitration award otherwise obtained may with the consent of all the parties interested be taken into consideration as a compromise or adjustment of a suit by any court before which the suit is pending."

Other secondary principles were developed by courts under the 1940 Act—to the effect that the arbitral tribunal was the final arbiter on facts—both as to the quantity and quality of the evidence produced before it under the 1940 Act. Even when it could be shown that an arbitrator had acted contrary to law, but this did not appear on the face of the award, the award (it was held) could not be set aside.

21. However, in an earlier decision *Allen Berry & Co.* vs. *Union of India* 1971 (3) SCR 282 at page 288, a document though referred to in the award was not regarded as incorporated in it since it was not annexed to it.
22. Citing *Indu Engineering* (2001), and stating as to how and when an arbitrator as arbitrator can go wrong: "He is a creature of contract between the parties and if he ignores the specific term of the contract, it would be a question of jurisdictional error which can be corrected by the court. A deliberate departure or conscious disregard of the contract not only manifests misconduct on his part, but it may tantamount to legal mala fide as well. It is further settled law that the arbitrator is not a conciliator and cannot ignore the law or misapply it in order to do what he thinks is just and reasonable."
23. The entire text of the New York Convention 1958, has been reproduced as the First Schedule to the Arbitration and Conciliation Act No. 26 of 1996.
24. Repealed by the provisions of the 1996 Act.

25. "Section 9. Saving. Nothing in this Act shall:
    (a). . .
    (b) apply to any award made on an arbitration agreement governed by the law of India."
26. For instance, Dicey, Morris & Collins: *Conflict of Laws*, Vol.I, 15th Edn., Sweet & Maxwell, London, 2012, p. 874, cites the decision of the Privy Council in *L. Oppenheim*.
27. Oppenheim's case was followed by the High Court of Calcutta in *John Batt and Co. London Ltd.* vs. *Kanoolal & Co.*, AIR 1926 Cal. 938 at page 941 (A similar view was taken by the High Court of Punjab in AIR 1958 Punjab 258, 260).
28. *Chanbasappa Hiremath* vs. *Basalingayya Hiremath:* I. L. R. (1927) 51 Bombay 908 (F.B.) = AIR 1927 Bom 565, 568. (F.B.).
29. (1934) 36 Bom. Law Reporter 47 = 150 Indian Cases 978 (D. B.) A similar view had been earlier taken by the High Court of Calcutta—a decision reported in ILR (1881) 6 Cal. 251).
30. See *Moolchand* vs. *Rashid Jamshed Sons and Co.* AIR 1946 Mad 840; *Ratanji Virpal* vs. *Dhirajlal Manilal* AIR 1942 Bom 101.; *Narbadabai And Ors.* Vs. *Natverlal*–AIR 1953 Bom. 386
31. See *National Ability S.A.* vs. *Tinna Oils and Chemicals Ltd.* (The Amazon Reefer) 2010 (1) Lloyd Law Report 222 para 5 (Court of Appeal). This is now possible also under India's 1996 Act (Section 51: Savings Clause in Part-II.)
32. Omitted in the title because Article-II of the New York Convention was formulated and put in place on the very last day of the conference in New York in June 1958.
33. The three enactments stand repealed by Section 85 of the Arbitration and Conciliation Act, 1996.

34. All of those enactments stand repealed by Section 85 of the Arbitration and Conciliation Act, 1996.
35. AIR 1959 S.C. 1357 (Bench of 3 judges)—it arose from a suit filed in the Calcutta High Court in November 1951.
36. 1955 (1) ILR Calcutta 29.
37. The view taken was that under the common law, a London award (not governed by any international convention) could be enforced by a suit in India had been also expressed in the decision of the Supreme Court of India in the case of *Badat & Co* vs. *East India Company reported in AIR 1964 S.C. 538;* English common law had been held (by a Bench of 9 judges of the Supreme Court of India) to be "law in force" under Article 372 of India's 1950 Constitution and therefore continued after 26 January 1950: See Superintendent & Legal Remembrancer, *State of West Bengal* vs. *Corporation of Calcutta*—1967 (2) SCR 170 (9 judges) at pages 186-187.
38. In *Badat*, the dissenting judge (Subba Rao who was the presiding judge) agreed with the decision of the Bombay High Court reported in AIR 1959 Bom. 414 (D. B.) which had relied on a passage in the Privy Council opinion in *Oppenheim*'s case (1922)—viz. that a foreign award does not always merge in the foreign judgment on award; Justice Subba Rao had held that the suit on the New York Award was maintainable and could be decreed.
39. The umpire was required to finally decide the reference to arbitration when the two arbitrators disagreed (under the First Schedule to the 1940 Act).
40. Under the Arbitration Act 1940 (Sec. 30), an award could be set aside by a civil court if the court found an error of law occurring on the face of the award (or in a document annexed to the award). This was established English law at the time following the old English case of *Hodgkinson* vs. *Fernie* reported in (1857) 140 ER 712

41. Gary Born: *International Commercial Arbitration*, Vol.-II (Second Edition), Kluwer Law International, Netherlands, 2010, Pp. 2411-2414, who described the decision as "idiosyncratic", had also stated that "the rationale adopted (by India's Supreme Court) in *National Thermal Power Corporation* stands alone, no other legal system has adopted such an aggressively nationalistic posture".

    In Redfern and Hunter: *International Arbitration*, 6th Edition, Oxford University Press, USA, 2014, at pages 639-640 the observations of the authors have been more sympathetic:

    > "Courts are not always immune to such creative attempts to resist enforcement. The Indian Supreme Court, for example, has in the past accepted that an award rendered in London that was the object of enforcement proceedings in the United States, could be set aside in India simply because the parties had chosen Indian law to govern the substance of their dispute. This type of decision is very much the exception that proves the rule, and the Indian Supreme Court itself has subsequently recognised this. Thus, in its decision of 2012, in *Bharat Aluminum Co.* vs. *Kaiser Aluminum Technical Service Inc.,* the Indian Supreme Court affirmed that Indian courts have no jurisdiction, in either a supportive or supervisory role, where the seat of arbitration is outside India."

2

Preparatory Steps

Enacting the Arbitration and Conciliation Act, 1996[1]

Adoption by India of the UNCITRAL Model Law 1985[2]*.*

The Asian African Legal Consultative Committee (AALCC)—of which 32 states were members (including India)—at its meeting held at Kuala Lumpur, Malaysia (30 June to 5 July, 1976)— considered the UNCITRAL Arbitration Rules that had been approved by the Commission, and invited UNCITRAL (United Nations Commission on International Trade Law) to consider the possibility of preparing a protocol to be annexed to the New York Convention 1958, and also, alternatively, the possibility of preparing a new international convention or a uniform law of arbitration including international commercial arbitration. Later, the AALCC was of the unanimous view that it would be in the interest of international commercial arbitration if UNCITRAL initiated steps for the establishment of uniform standards of arbitral procedures and that the preparation of a model law on arbitration was the most appropriate way to achieve the desired uniformity. The Commission later agreed that there was no need to revise the New York Convention or adopt a new protocol for it, but that it would be advisable to prepare a model arbitration law to assist states in reforming and modernising their laws and to this end the Commission requested the secretariat to prepare—in consultation with interested international organisations, in particular the Asian African Legal Consultative Committee

(AALCC) and the International Council for Commercial Arbitration (ICCA)—a preliminary draft of a "Model Law on Arbitral Procedures". It was decided that the draft should be restricted to international commercial arbitration and should not attempt to deal with domestic arbitration, and it should take into account the provisions of the New York Convention 1958 and the UNCITRAL Arbitration Rules.

The Commission then decided to proceed to draft a model law and to entrust the task to its existing Working Group on International Contract Practices[3]. It requested the secretariat to prepare background-studies and a draft text to assist the Working Group. Ultimately the draft text of the Model Law was prepared, India's representative stating that India was satisfied with the draft text, but that it should be discussed by the Commission in plenary meetings since member states were more broadly represented at such meetings. The draft text of the Model Law on International Commercial Arbitration was then transmitted to all governments, and interested international organisations, for their comments. Later, in the Summary Report of Proceedings of 3 June 1985, India's representative stated that his country's participation in the work of a Model Law on International Commercial Arbitration was in the best spirit of its own Constitution (i.e. the Constitution of India 1950) which contained a Directive Principle calling for international disputes to be settled by arbitration.

Ultimately, on 21 June 1985, the Commission, after much discussion, and after consideration of the text of the draft model law as revised by the Drafting Group, decided to adopt the UNCITRAL Model Law on International

Commercial Arbitration, and invited the General Assembly to recommend to states that they should consider the Model Law when they enact or revise their laws to meet current needs of International Commercial Arbitration. On 11 December 1985, the General Assembly of the United Nations passed the following Resolution:

General Assembly Resolution 40/72 A/40/53 (11 December 1985)

40/72. Model Law on International Commercial Arbitration of the United Nations Commission on International Trade Law

The General Assembly

Recognising the value of arbitration as a method of settling disputes arising in international commercial relations.

Being convinced that establishment of a Model Law on arbitration that is acceptable to states with different legal, social and economic systems contributes to the development of harmonious international economic relations.

Noting that the Model Law on International Commercial Arbitration was adopted by the United Nations Commission on International Trade Law at its eighteenth session, after due deliberation and extensive consultation with arbitral institutions and individual experts on international commercial arbitration.

Being convinced that the Model Law, together with the Convention on the Recognition and Enforcement of Foreign arbitral awards and the Arbitration Rules of the United Nations Commission on International Trade Law, recommended by the General Assembly in its resolution 31/98 of 15 December 1976, significantly contributes to the establishment of a unified legal framework for the fair and efficient settlement of disputes arising in international commercial relations.

1. *Requests* the Secretary-General to transmit the text of the Model Law on International Commercial Arbitration of the United Nations Commission on International Trade Law, together with the *travaux preparatoires* from the eighteenth session of the Commission, to governments and the arbitral institutions and other interested bodies, such as chambers of commerce;
2. *Recommends* that all states give due consideration to the Model Law on International Commercial Arbitration, in view of the desirability of uniformity of the law of arbitral procedures and the specific needs of international commercial arbitration practice.

***

After the introduction of India's New Economic Policy (1991)[4] involving liberalisation of the economy, there was a growing demand of the business community and of international investors for reforms in the Indian legal system especially arbitration law, to make it an attractive avenue for business investments. The Chief Ministers Conference and Chief Justices Conference of December

1993, had set up working groups to tackle the problem of arrears of cases in courts and tribunals using alternative means of dispute resolution such as arbitration, mediation and negotiation[5].

In September 1994, the Law Ministers' Working Group proposed a new unified arbitration law for resolving national and international trade disputes through arbitration and conciliation instead of by litigation. The government had many international models[6] from which to choose and it chose the UNCITRAL Model Law of International Commercial Arbitration, 1985[7] as well as the UNCITRAL Conciliation Rules, 1980 which harmonised both common law and civil law approaches to arbitration and were universal in application. The UNCITRAL Model Law on International Commercial Arbitration, 1985 (UNCITRAL Model Law) had prescribed judicial non-intervention in arbitral proceedings (Article 5) and affirmed party autonomy with regard to arbitral procedures (Article 19(1) and 19(2))[8]. It also provided for judicial assistance to the arbitral process in the form of provisional measures, the constitution of an arbitral tribunal and procedure for taking of evidence (Articles 9, 11 to 13 and 27).

The following developed and developing nations had enacted laws on the basis of the UNCITRAL Model Law[9], for promoting international consistency between international and national domestic arbitral regimes: viz. Canada[10] (and separately) the province of British Colombia in Canada, Cyprus[11], Bulgaria[12], Nigeria[13], California[14] (the largest state in the USA), Australia[15] and Hong Kong[16], the states of Connecticut[17] and of Texas (in the USA)[18]; Scotland[19]; Peru[20]; Bermuda[21], the Russian Federation[22],

Mexico[23], Tunisia[24], the Ukraine[25], Egypt[26], Bahrain[27], Hungary[28], Singapore[29], Kenya[30], Guatemala[31], Sri Lanka[32], Brazil[33], India[34], Lithuania,[35] Malta[36], Zimbabwe[37] and New Zealand[38].

***

The Working Group in India had before it three separate adaptations of the UNCITRAL Model Law, 1985.

(a) Adoption of the UNCITRAL Model law and its incorporation: Countries like Canada (Federal), Australia, and Hong Kong have adopted the Model Law attaching it to their respective national laws;
(b) Adaptation of the UNCITRAL Model Law: Countries like the Netherlands[39] and the United Kingdom[40] which did not adopt the Model Law, took special care to make their own national law compatible with it; and
(c) *Adopting* many of the provisions of the Model Law and *adapting* some other provisions with amendments. In territories like the province of British Columbia (1986) in Canada, and the state of California in the USA, legislation was framed based principally on the UNCITRAL Model Law, but using the local drafting format for giving effect to many of the provisions of the Model Law.

***

Item (c) above was chosen in the new draft of India's Arbitration and Conciliation Bill which was prepared by the late Dr P. Chandrasekhara Rao[41], Secretary (Legal Affairs) in the Ministry of Law and Justice. The first Part (now Part-I of the proposed new law) was based primarily on the pattern of the International Commercial Arbitration Act, 1986 of British Columbia, which had adopted the language of the UNCITRAL Model Law formatted on the Canadian pattern.[42] In its judgment in 1992, Canada's Supreme Court had recognised the enforcement of dispute resolution-provisions (in the Model Law) as facilitating the pursuit of freer trade on an international scale.[43]

The new Draft Bill was extensively considered by the Working Group of law ministers from nine different states or bodies, by arbitral institutions, by representatives of industries and by legal experts aligning the Indian laws with international laws—mainly to prevent un-called for judicial interference in arbitration matters. The first meeting of the Law Minister's Working Group was held on 4 to 6 October 1994, at Bombay on the Draft Bill (known as the 'Bombay Draft') when Dr P. C. Rao stated:

> To make arbitration a success story in India, we need three things: a good law that is responsive to our needs; honest and impartial arbitrators without whom any law can be frustrated; and the litigants, particularly the commercial community that is willing to play the game in good faith. We are currently engaged in the task of projecting a new, and hopefully good law. We need to attend to other parts soon.[44]

Meetings of the Working Group (in India) were then held in Chandigarh (capital of the states of Punjab and Haryana) on 31 October 1994, in New Delhi on 5 November 1994 and in Calcutta (now Kolkata) on 15 and 17 November, 1994, where a 'Calcutta Draft' (largely following the Bombay Draft) was prepared incorporating a few more suggestions. Finally, in December 1994 and January 1995, the Working Group prepared a revised draft— Arbitration and Conciliation Bill, 1995—which inter-alia had stated its objective of minimising the supervisory role of the courts in the arbitral process, and therefore provided that every final arbitral award be enforced in the same manner as if it were a decree of the court. It comprehensively covered in one law: International Commercial Arbitration and other Domestic Arbitration (Part-I), foreign (arbitral) Awards and New York Convention Awards (Part-II) and Conciliation (Part-III).

***

In May 1995, the Arbitration and Conciliation Bill, 1995 was introduced in the Rajya Sabha (the Upper House of India's Parliament). At a time when Parliament was not in session, the President of India first promulgated the Arbitration and Conciliation Ordinance, 1996 (on 25 January 1996) under Article 123(1) of India's Constitution[45]. Its provisions were almost identical to the Arbitration and Conciliation Bill, 1995. The Arbitration & Conciliation Ordinance had to be promulgated once again in March 1996, and yet again a third time in June 1996, because of the dissolution of the Lok Sabha—the lower house of India's Parliament and the calling of General Elections in April and May 1996. Finally, in August 1996, the newly elected (Lok Sabha) Parliament passed the

Arbitration and Conciliation Bill, which, after presidential ascent became the Arbitration and Conciliation Act No. 26 of 1996, which was notified to be in force as from 22 August 1996 (vide CoSR 375th)—the date appointed by the Government of India.

After the Amending Act No. 3 of 2016 was passed, amending the provisions of the Arbitration and Conciliation Act, 1996, the Government of India set up a high level committee (available at: http://legalaffairs.gov.in/sites/default/files/Report-HLC.pdf), under the chairmanship of retired Justice B. N. Srikrishna, (former judge of the Supreme Court of India) to examine the effectiveness of the existing mechanism by studying the functioning and performance of arbitration institutions in India and to devise a roadmap of institutional arbitration in India. The committee submitted its report on 30 July 2017, recommending the establishment of an independent body for grading arbitral institutions and for the accreditation of arbitrators. It also recommended certain amendments to the 1996 Act (as already amended) to minimise the need to approach courts for appointment of arbitrators and made further recommendations "to enable India to become a hub of institutional arbitration for both domestic and international arbitration."

The recommendations of this committee were incorporated in the Arbitration and Conciliation Amendment Bill No. 100 of 2018, which though passed in the Lok Sabha in August 2018, lapsed since it could not be moved in and passed by the Rajya Sabha (council of states) because of the dissolution of the Lok Sabha on the expiry of its five year term in May 2019.

After the general elections of May 2019, the provisions of the Arbitration and Conciliation Amendment Bill of 2018, were re-introduced as The Arbitration and Conciliation (Amendment) Bill. No: XXI of 2019. The bill was passed both by the Lok Sabha and the Rajya Sabha on 18 July 2019, and with presidential assent has now became the Arbitration and Conciliation (Amendment) Act No. 33 of 2019.

The salient features of the Arbitration and Conciliation (Amendment) Act No. 33 of 2019, are as follows:

(1) to amend section 11 of the Act relating to "Appointment of Arbitrators" so as to change the present system of appointment of arbitrators by the Supreme Court or high courts, to a system where the arbitrators shall be appointed by the "arbitral institutions" designated by the Supreme Court or High Courts;
(2) in case where no graded arbitral institutions are available, the Chief Justice of the concerned high court may maintain a panel of arbitrators for discharging the functions and duties of arbitral institutions;
(3) to insert a new Part 1A to the 1996 Act for the establishment and incorporation of an independent body namely, the Arbitration Council of India for the purpose of grading of arbitral institutions and accreditation of arbitrators, etc.;
(4) to amend Section 11 of the principal Act (the Arbitration and Conciliation Act, 1996) providing for the power of the Supreme Court and the high courts to designate arbitral institutions from time

to time which have been graded by the Arbitration Council of India; also to amend Sections 17, 23, 29A, 34 and 37 of the principal Act (the Arbitration and Conciliation Act, 1996) and to add to the principal Act Sections 42A (Confidentiality of Information) and Section 42B (Protection of Action Taken in Good Faith);

(5) to clarify that Section 26 of the Arbitration and Conciliation (Amendment) Act, 2015 (Act No. 3 of 2016), (Act not to apply its pending arbitral proceedings) is applicable only to the arbitral proceedings which commenced on or after 23 October 2015, and to such court proceedings which emanate from such arbitral proceedings.

(6) What is referred hereafter in the book as the '1996 Act' includes not only the Act as enacted but also the additions/deletions effected by the Amending Act No.3 of 2016 as well as the Amending Act No.33 of 2019.

End Notes:

1. Act 26 of 1996 was amended—in several parts—by Amending Act 3 of 2016, following the recommendations made by the Law Commission of India in its 246th Report (August 2014); (available at: (http://lawcommissionofindia.nic.in/reports/Report246.pdf). Later in December 2016, a high level Committee was appointed by the Government of India to review the institutionalisation of arbitration

mechanism in India (available at: (http://legalaffairs.gov.in/sites/default/files/Report-HLC.pdf). The committee presented its report to the Government of India in July 2017, which is in three parts:

Part-I of the report contained the committee's findings on "Institutional Arbitration in India."

Part-II of the report contained a study of the working and performance of the International Centre for Alternative Disputes Resolution (ICADR) and the committee's recommendations for its reform.

Part-III of the report dealt with The Role of Arbitrations in BIT disputes involving the Union of India and the committee's recommendations on the same.

The recommendations in Part-I and Part-II of its report and its recommendation for some more amendments of provisions of the then existing Arbitration and Conciliation Act, 1996 (as amended) has been adopted by the Arbitration and Conciliation (Amendment) Bill No. 21 of 2019 passed by both Houses of Parliament in July 2019, principally to incorporate Part-IA in the 1996 Act, with provisions for establishing an Arbitration Council of India and for prescribing the duties of and functions of such a council, along with a few recommended amendments to the 1996 Act. This is now the Arbitration and Conciliation Amendment Act No. 33_2019. No decision has yet been taken on Part-III of the report.

2. India became a party to UNCITRAL in 1966 and a representative of India was a member of the Working Group of UNCITRAL that drafted the Model Law 1985 and helped shape its final outcome. The United Nations Commission on International Trade law (UNCITRAL) adopted the UNCITRAL Model Law on International Commercial Arbitration in 1985.

3. The following states were members of the Group: Austria, Czechoslovakia, France, Ghana, Guatemala, Hungary, India, Japan, Kenya, Philippines, Sierra Leone, Trinidad and Tobago, Union of Soviet Socialist Republics (USSR), United Kingdom of Great Britain and Northern Islands (UK) and United States of America (USA).
4. India's New Economic Policy dated 24 July 1991. https://www.iasscore.in/pdf/Globalization.pdf
5. http://en.wikimediation.org/index.php?title=International_Center_for_Alternative_Dispute_Resolution_(ICADR)
6. As stated in a commentary by Dr P. C. Rao: *The Arbitration and Conciliation Act, 1996*, Universal Publications, India, 1997, Pp. 8-9.
7. With amendments adopted by UNCITRAL later in the year 2006 (taking effect in 2010).
8. The secretariat of UNCITRAL observed that Article 19 is "the Magna Carta" of arbitral procedure (Seventh Secretariat Note (25-03-1985): *Guide to the Model Law*, 1985, Pp. 582-583: cited in Howard Holtzmann and Joseph Neuhans: *A Guide to the UNCITRAL Model Law on International Commercial Arbitratio*n, Kluwer Law International, Netherlands, 1989, p. 564: "It goes a long way towards establishing procedural autonomy by recognising the parties' freedom to lay down the rules of procedure". Also, Article 18 of the Model Law states that, "the parties shall be treated with equality and each party shall be given a full opportunity of presenting his case."
9. Till February 2019, 80 countries to the UNCITRAL Model Law have enacted legislation based on the UNCITRAL Model-law, 1985. See.www.uncitral.org/unictral/en/uncitral_texts/arbitration/1985modellaw_arbitration_status.html

10. Canada: *The Statutes of Canada*, 1986, chapter 22, contains the Commercial Arbitration Act, S.C. 1986, C 92 (based on UNCITRAL Model Law). It omitted the word "international" in the first para of Article-I and deleted paras 3 and 4. The code applies to commercial arbitrations whether international or domestic (all part of one regime).

    British Columbia: enacted the International Commercial Arbitration Act S.B.C. 1986, C. 14 17-06-1986 (with certain adjustments to UNCITRAL Model Law).

    India: has based Part-I of its 1996 Arbitration and Conciliation Bill, on the law of British Colombia.
11. Cyprus: The International Commercial Arbitration Law, 1987 (mostly based on Model Law only).
12. Bulgaria: The Law on International Commercial Arbitration (State Gazette No. 60 of 5 August 1988). It is based on the basic ideas, principles of the Model Law and applies to domestic arbitration also.
13. Nigeria: The Arbitration Decree of 1988, is also based on UNCITRAL Model Law.
14. California (USA): Arbitration and Conciliation of International Commercial Disputes, California Division Procedure Code Sec. 1297.11 to 1297.432 (w.e.f. 7 March 1988) (adopted the Model Law with modification and copied the British Columbia ICA Act, 1986 to large extent).
15. Australia: The International Arbitration Amendment Act, 1989 amended the Arbitration (Foreign Awards and Agreements) Act, 1974 by omitting "Arbitration (foreign Awards and Agreements) "and substituting "International Arbitration", repealed Sections 5, 6 and 11 and after section 14, inserted Part-III International Commercial Arbitration (section 15 to section 30) and Schedule- II (adopting the whole of the UNCITRAL Model Law).

16. Hong Kong: Arbitration Ordinance Chapter 341 (Revised in October 1990 created two separate arbitration regimes: (1) Part-II based on English Law for Domestic Arbitration (2) Part-IIA based on the UNCITRAL Model Law for International Arbitration, (Under Sections 2L and 2M: parties can opt in writing to adopt either domestic or international regimes).
17. Connecticut (USA): The UNCITRAL Model Law on International Commercial Arbitration was adopted as it is Publ. Act 89-179, 1989, Connecticut Legislation. Serv. 26 (West) was approved on 1 June 1989, based on Model Law.
18. Texas (USA): Arbitration and Conciliation of International Disputes, Tex. Rev. Cir. Stat. Ann. Articles 249-1 to 249-43 (1 September 1989). Similar to the (California) International Arbitration Law, 1986.
19. Scotland: Law Reform (Miscellaneous provisions) Scotland Act, 1990—Section 66 (2) and Schedule 7 contains a modified form of the UNCITRAL Model Law with Section 66(4): an opting-in clause).
20. Peru: Decree Law No. 25935 of 1992 (General Arbitration Law). Section 1: Domestic Arbitration (Articles 1 to 80); Section 2: International Arbitration (Article 81-109), (Article 82 makes the provisions of Section 1 applicable to Section 2 "on a supplementary basis"); it closely follows UNCITRAL Model Law.
21. Bermuda: The Bermuda International Conciliation and Arbitration Act, 1993 has adopted the Model Law with modifications: under Section 29 but parties can contract out of the Model Law.
22. Russian Federation: Law of the Russian Federation on International Commercial Arbitration (August 1993) has taken into account the UNCITRAL Model Law.

23. Mexico: Decree dated 22 July 1993, Commercial Code, Title-IV (of Book V) follows the UNCITRAL Model Law very closely, but not verbatim. It is geared to International Commercial Arbitration; Article 1415 states that the new law applies to domestic arbitration as well.
24. Tunisia: The Arbitration Code (October 1993), Chapter-III (Article 47-82) International Commercial Arbitration is largely based on the UNCITRAL Model Law.
25. Ukraine: The Law of Ukraine on International Commercial Arbitration (24 February 1994) has adopted the UNCITRAL Model Law.
26. Egypt: Law No: 27/1994: The law concerning arbitration in civil and commercial matters, is based on the UNCITRAL Model Law but applies to both domestic and international arbitration.
27. Bahrain: Decree No. 9 of 1994: 'The International Commercial Arbitration Law'.
28. Hungary: The Arbitration Act LXXI of 1994. It applies the UNCITRAL Model Law to domestic and international arbitration.
29. Singapore: International Arbitration Act, 1994, is based largely on the UNCITRAL Model Law. It applies to international arbitration, but parties to domestic arbitration may "opt into" its regime and conversely parties to an international arbitration may agree to "opt out" of its regime.
30. Kenya: The Arbitration Act No. 4 of 1995 has adapted the UNCITRAL Model Law with modification. It applies to domestic and international arbitration.
31. Guatemala: The Arbitration Law (Decree 67-95) is based on the UNCITRAL Model Law with modifications, and applies to national and international arbitration.
32. Sri Lanka: Sri Lanka Arbitration Act No. 11 of 1995 follows to a large extent the UNCITRAL Model Law. It applies to all arbitration proceedings conducted in Sri Lanka.

33. Brazil: the Brazilian Arbitration Act, 1996
34. India: The Arbitration and Conciliation Act, 1996 is based largely on the UNCITRAL Model Law with the British Columbia International Commercial Arbitration Act, 1986 taken as the Model.
35. Lithuania: The Law of Commercial Arbitration, 1996 is based on the UNCITRAL Model Law.
36. Malta: The Arbitration Act-II of 1996 (Chapter 387) is based largely on the UNCITRAL Model Law.
37. Zimbabwe: The Arbitration Act 6 of 1996 applies the Model Law with modifications: the UNCITRAL Model Law applies to both domestic and international arbitration.
38. New Zealand: The Arbitration Act, 1996 (w.e.f. 1 July 1997) applies the UNCITRAL Model Law to both domestic and international arbitration.
39. The Netherlands Arbitration Act (1 December 1986) Code of Civil Procedure —Book Four—Arbitration. Title one: *Arbitration in Netherlands*; Title two: *Arbitration outside the Netherlands*.
40. The English Arbitration Act, 1996 (Chapter 23).
    Case Law on the UNCITRAL Model Law (CLOUT—*Case Law on Uncitral Texts: A legal database of worldwide court decisions and arbitral awards on UNCITRAL texts*) in the form of extracts of decisions of courts in states that have adopted or adapted the Model Law, is also readily available on https://www.uncitral.org/uncitral/en/case_law.html
41. Dr P. C. Rao was also a member of the International Tribunal Law of the Sea from 1996 to 1999 and then its president from 1999 to 2002.
42. It had been so stated by the draftsman of the Bill, P. Chandrashekhar Rao, Secretary, Ministry of Law, in his published commentary on the Act: (soon after the 1996 Act was enacted):

"While drafting the Act, the International Commercial Arbitration Act, 1986, of British Columbia was taken as a model, for it conformed largely to the Indian drafting style. Though the drafting style of the Act differs from that of the Model Law, the Act retains the language of the Model Law to the extent possible." (See a *Commentary on the Arbitration and Conciliation Act, 1996* Universal Law Publishing Co. Pvt. Ltd., Delhi, page 9).

The British Columbia Act on International Commercial Arbitration, 1996 is readily available on:

http://www.bclaws.ca/civix/document/id/complete/statreg/96233_01 and cases of Canadian courts decided under this Act (and its later amendment) are also available on CLOUT (*Case Law on Uncitral Texts:* A legal database of worldwide court decisions and arbitral awards on UNCITRAL texts) https://www.uncitral.org/uncitral/en/case_law.html

43. *Kaverit Steel* vs. *Craine Ltd.*, a 1992 decision of the Supreme Court of Canada reported in 1992 (87) *Dominion Law Reports*, 4th Edition 129, page 139.
44. Unpublished Draft papers of the draft Arbitration and Conciliation Bill, 1995.
45. Article 123 (1) of the Constitution of India, 1950 reads as follows:

"If at any time, except when both Houses of Parliament are in session, the President is satisfied that circumstances exist which render it necessary for him to take immediate action, he may promulgate such ordinances as the circumstances appear to him to require."

3

Words of Caution

Old Laws vs. New Laws

Before analysing and commenting on the provisions in Part-I, (along with Part-IA), Part-II and Part-III of the Arbitration and Conciliation Act 26, of 1996 (as amended by Amending Act 3 of 2016 and further amended by both houses of Parliament in July, 2019) a few preliminary *words of caution* are necessary—they are summarised below, and elaborated later:

(i) The old laws of arbitration—and of court decisions under them—have to be ignored when interpreting or applying the Act of 1996 (*as enacted, and as later amended in 2016 and 2019)*;

(ii) In interpreting and applying the 1996 Act, no provision in Part-I (Sections 2 to 43) can be made applicable to Part-II (NYC Awards),[1] although for an entire decade (2002-2012) the contrary had been decided by the Supreme Court of India (in 2002) by a Bench decision of 3 judges—a decision overruled by a Bench of 5 judges only in 2012;

(iii) A key feature of the UNCITRAL Model Law, 1985 is the principle of judicial non-intervention. However, decided cases have shown that this is only an aspiration, because in India; judicial non-intervention mandated by Section 5 of the Act, is not observed too strictly by the courts;

(iv) In matters relating to arbitrability of a dispute there has been a discernible trend in India for courts to narrow (rather than to couden) the range of disputes that are capable of being submitted to arbitration.

(v) There have been far too many amendments to the 1996 Act – resulting in some confusion and inconsistencies in the law.

***

Re(i)—*The old laws of arbitration—and of court decisions under them—are to be ignored when interpreting or applying the Act of 1996 (as enacted and as later amended by Amending) in 2016 and 2019).*

When interpreting or attempting to analyse or apply all or any of the provisions of the current Indian law of arbitration, it is most important not to recall former provisions of law (relating to arbitration) nor as to how such provisions were interpreted or applied by the courts—not even by the Supreme Court of India. Cases under the old laws of arbitration (including the cases under the Arbitration Act of 1940) keep getting reported in the law reports after (in fact, long after) the year 1996. This is only because of time taken in India's three-tier system of court proceedings and the law's inevitable delays. Such cases, decided under the 1940 Act, are no longer relevant since the cases so reported (originating pre-1996) are under the old Indian law of arbitration. This is not just a friendly word of warning; it has been emphasised by the Supreme Court of India. In *Sundaram Finance* vs. *NEPC India Ltd.* reported in 1999 (2) SCC 479, the court authoritatively said:

> "The 1996 Act is very different from the Arbitration Act 1940. The provisions of this Act have, therefore,

to be interpreted and construed independently and, in fact, reference to the 1940 Act, may actually lead to misconstruction. In other words, the provisions of 1996 Act have to be interpreted uninfluenced by the principles underlying the 1940 Act. In order to get help in construing these provisions it is more relevant to refer to the UNCITRAL Model Law rather than the 1940 Act."[3]

Fourteen years later, in *Chloro Controls Pvt. Ltd.* vs. *Severn Trent Water Purification* (3 judges) 2013 (1) SCC 641 (at para 62), India's Supreme Court once again stated:

> "The 1996 Act makes it abundantly clear that Part-I of the Act has been amended to bring these provisions in line with the UNCITRAL Model Law, while Chapter-I of P-II is meant to encourage international commercial arbitration by incorporating in India the provisions of the New York Convention[4]."

In *Purushottam, s/o Tulsiram Badwai* vs. *Anil and Ors.* reported in 2018 (8) SCC 95 it has been held that wherever there is an arbitration agreement which satisfies the requirements of Section 7 of the 1996 Act, and if no arbitral proceeding has been commenced before the Act came into force "the matter would be *completely governed by the provisions of 1996 Act. Any reference to the 1940 Act, in the arbitration agreement would be of no consequence and the matter would be referred to arbitration only in terms of the 1996 Act, consistent with the basic intent of the parties as discernible from the Arbitration Agreement to refer the dispute to arbitration.*"

***

Re: (ii)—*In interpreting the 1996 Act, no provision in Part-I (Sections 2 to 43) can be made to apply to Part-II (New York Convention Awards)*[5]*, however for a decade (2002-2012) the contrary had been decided by the Supreme Court of India (in the year 2002) by a Bench decision of 3 judges—a decision overruled by a Bench of 5 judges only in the year 2012.*

In 2002 the law declared by a Bench of 3 judges of the Supreme Court of India in *Bhatia International* vs. *Bulk Trading*[6] was that the provisions of Part-I—Arbitration (Section 2 to 43)—adopting the UNCITRAL Model Law of 1985—could be also invoked and made applicable to the provisions of Chapter I of Part-II Section 44 to 52, (Foreign Awards—New York Convention Awards)—especially (according to the court's decision in *Bhatia*) because of the omission of the word "only" in Section 2(2) of the 1996 Act: when contrasted with Article 1(2) of the Model Law wherein it had been stated:

> "The provisions of the law" (i.e. the entire Model Law) except Articles 8, 9, 35 and 36[7] apply *only* if the place of arbitration is in the territory of India."

(The word "only" had been omitted in Section 2(2) of the 1996 Act). According to India's Constitution (Article 141) the law declared by the Supreme Court of India is binding on all courts in the country (and even on co-ordinate benches of the Supreme Court of India), which consistently followed the law declared in *Bhatia*.

However, *Bhatia* was ultimately overruled (ten years later) by a Constitution Bench decision of five judges in

Bharat Aluminium Co. (*Balco*) vs. *Kaiser Aluminium*[8] (2012) 9 SCC 552. The conclusion in *Balco* (2012—Bench of 5 judges)—was as follows:

> "194. In view of the above discussion, we are of the considered opinion that the Arbitration Act, 1996 has accepted the territoriality principle which has been adopted in the UNCITRAL Model Law. Section 2(2) makes a declaration that Part-I of the Arbitration Act, 1996 shall apply to all arbitrations which take place within India. *We are of the considered opinion that Part-I of the Arbitration Act, 1996 would have no application to International Commercial Arbitration held outside India.* Therefore, such awards would only be subject to the jurisdiction of the Indian courts when the same are sought to be enforced in India in accordance with the provisions contained in Part-II of the Arbitration Act, 1996. In our opinion, the provisions contained in the Arbitration Act, 1996 make it crystal clear that there can be no overlapping or intermingling of the provisions contained in Part-I with the provisions contained in Part-II of the Arbitration Act, 1996.
>
> 195. . .
>
> 196. *We conclude that Part-I of the Arbitration Act, 1996 is applicable only to all the arbitrations which take place within the territory of India.* (emphasis added)."

In Redfern and Hunter: *International Arbitration*, 6th Edition, published by Oxford University Press, US, the change in Indian judicial thinking has been stated as follows:[9]

> "... in the 2002 case *Bhatia International* vs. *Bulk Trading S.A.* which confirmed the supervisory jurisdiction of the Indian courts in certain circumstances in which the seat was not in India, had been followed by the Indian Supreme Court's 2008 decision in *Venture Global* vs. *Satyam Trading*, in which the court set aside an award rendered in England on the basis that Indian law governed the substance of the dispute. Decisions such as these appeared to indicate that the Indian courts were free to intervene in arbitrations that had their seat outside of India wherever Indian law governed the merits of the dispute. The Supreme Court of India has since reversed course in 2012, in its Constitutional Court formation, (of a Bench of 5 judges) in *Bharat Aluminium Co.* (*Balco*) vs. *Kaiser Aluminium Technical Services*, in which it overturned *Venture Global* and confirmed the international practice that the power to set aside is limited to the courts of the seat of the arbitration."[10]

In *Bharat Aluminium Co.* (*Balco*), the Supreme Court (Bench of 5 judges) had added one last paragraph to its judgment which read:

> "197. The judgment in Bhatia International (supra) was rendered by this Court on 13th March, 2002. Since, then, the aforesaid judgment has been followed by all the High Courts as well as by this Court on

numerous occasions. In fact, the judgment in Venture Global Engineering (supra) has been rendered on 10th January, 2008 in terms of the ratio of the decision in Bhatia International (supra). Thus, in order to do complete justice, we hereby order, that the law now declared by this Court shall apply prospectively, to all the artibration agreements executed hereafter."

This last paragraph quoted above placed in peril thousands of pending matters and pending arbitration agreements because despite *Bhatia* being overruled, those pending matters (only because of this paragraph) would remain governed by the (wrong) law previously declared in *Bhatia*! But, since the year 1977 a quietus has been given to the last paragraph (para 197) of the judgment in *Bharat Aluminium Co.* (quoted above), because of law declared by a subsequent judgment of the Supreme Court of India in *Union of India* vs. *Reliance Industries*[11] (2015), the relevant paragraph of which reads as follows:

"21. The last paragraph of *Bharat Aluminium Co's* judgment (2012) has now to be read with two caveats, both emanating from paragraph 32 of *Bhatia International* itself —that where the court comes to a determination that the juridical seat is outside India or where law, other than Indian law, governs the arbitration agreement, Part-I of the Arbitration Act, 1996 would be excluded by necessary implication. Therefore, even in the cases governed by the *Bhatia* principle, <u>it is only those cases in which agreements stipulate that the seat of the arbitration is in India or</u>

> on whose facts a judgment cannot be reached on the seat of the arbitration as being outside India that would continue to be governed by the *Bhatia* principle. Also, it is only those agreements which stipulate or can be read to stipulate that the law governing the arbitration agreement is Indian law which would continue to be governed by the *Bhatia* rule." (emphasis added)

So, despite, the last paragraph of the judgment in *Bharat Aluminium Co.* (*Balco*) (para 197) the settled law now is: *that where the seat of arbitration is outside India or where law other than Indian law governs the arbitration agreement, Part-I of the Act is excluded.* (emphasis added)

***

Re (iii)—*A key feature of the UNCITRAL Model Law, 1985 is the principle of judicial non-intervention. But decided cases have shown that this is only an aspiration. In India, judicial non-intervention mandated by Section 5 of the Act is observed by the courts—but not too strictly.*

Section 5 (Extent of judicial intervention), in Part I of the 1996 Act,[12] is based on Article 5 of the UNCITRAL Model Law.[13] The main object being "to minimise the supervisory role of the courts in the arbitral process[14]. The term "judicial authority" in Section 5 is important. It has a much wider connotation than the word "court" and therefore includes not merely the civil courts but other forums as well, like the Debt Recovery Tribunal, Consumer forums, etc.[15]

Over the years, Section 5 of the 1996 Act has been enforced (at times)—but (at other times) read down by courts as not affecting the *inherent powers* of the court. For example:

(a) In 2004, the High Court of Delhi in *Union of India* vs. *Dhabol Power Company* held that prima facie neither Section 5 (in Part-I) nor Section 45 (in Part-II) of the 1996 Act had ousted the jurisdiction of the court from issuing an injunction if it were found that the arbitral proceedings against the plaintiff in a foreign country were oppressive and called for Judicial interference.[16] The high court granted an interim injunction of stay (under Order 39 Rules-1 and 2 read with section 151 of CPC, 1908 of arbitral proceedings in London, while an appeal was pending before the Supreme Court of India. The proceedings in London were considered to be oppressive because the arbitrators there were seeking to proceed despite pendency of the appeal before India's Supreme Court. It was observed (by the Delhi High Court) that courts are not only courts of law but courts of equity as well.

(b) Section 22(1) and 22(3) of SICA (Sick Industrial Companies [Special Provisions] Act, 1985) had provided for a bar on enforcement and a suspension of arbitral awards (in proceedings instituted under this Act). But it was held by the Supreme Court of India in the year 2014, that since the provisions of SICA also contained a non-obstante clause it would override the non-obstante clause under section 5 of 1996 Act—because SICA "was enacted to give effect to a larger Public Interest" and "seeks to achieve a higher goal."[17] (SICA has since been repealed by the Insolvency and Bankruptcy Code of 2016).

(c) However, in another case, also decided in the year 2014, Section 5 was enforced. In *World Sport Group (Mauritius) Ltd.* vs. *MSM Satellite Singapore Pvt. Ltd.*[18]—section 5 was relied upon to keep the courts out of what parties had agreed should be decided by arbitration. When an arbitrable dispute arose between the parties, the appellant sent a request for arbitration to the International Chamber of Commerce (ICC), Paris (place of arbitration: Singapore) which in turn issued a notice to the respondent. The respondent then filed a suit in the Bombay High Court for a declaration that the Facilitation Deed (containing the arbitration clause) had stood rescinded and that the appellant was not entitled to invoke the arbitration clause. The respondent filed an application for temporary injunction in its pending suit restraining the appellant from continuing with the proceedings abroad under the aegis of the ICC. A single judge of the Bombay High Court rejected the application for temporary injunction holding that it would be for the arbitrator to decide whether the Facilitation Deed was void on account of fraud or misrepresentation as contended for by the respondent. On appeal, the Division Bench of the Bombay High Court set aside the single judge's order and granted the temporary injunction[19]. In granting special leave to appeal India's Supreme Court reversed the judgment of the Division Bench of the high court and restored the order of the single judge stating:

"34. This arbitration agreement in clause 9 is wide enough to bring this dispute within the scope of arbitration. To quote Redfern and Hunter on *International Arbitration* (Fifth edition, page 134 para 2.141):

> "Where allegations of fraud in the procurement or performance of a contract are alleged, there appears to be no reason for the arbitral tribunal to decline jurisdiction."

Hence, it had been rightly held by the learned single judge of the Bombay High Court that it is for the arbitrator to decide this dispute in accordance with the arbitration agreement."[20]

***

Re: (iv)—*In matters relating to arbitrability of a dispute there is a discernible trend in India for courts to narrow the range of disputes that are capable of being submitted to arbitration.*

The extent of "non-judicial intervention under section 5 of the Act has to be read along with section 2(3) of the Act (also in Part-I) which states:

> "This part shall not affect any other law for the time being force by virtue of which certain dispute may not be submitted to Arbitration."

The interpretation given by the Supreme Court of India from time to time to Section 2(3) has limited the concept of arbitrability rather than extended it.[21]

In the following decisions of the courts[22] the range of non-arbitrable disputes has been extended to include:

(i) disputes relating to rights and liabilities which give rise to or arise out of criminal offences;[23]

(ii) matrimonial disputes[24] relating to divorce, judicial separation, restitution of conjugal rights, child custody;

(iii) matters concerning guardianship;[25]

(iv) matters relating to insolvency and winding up of companies;[26]

(v) testamentary matters[27] (grant of probate, letters of administration and succession certificate);

(vi) certain disputes under the Consumer Protection Act, 1986;[28]

(vii) while dealing with the issue of arbitrability regarding allegations of fraud, in one questionable decision the Supreme Court of India has ruled that there is a distinction between "*serious* allegations of fraud" and "*mere* allegations of fraud" and courts would have to deal with the question of whether allegations are "*serious* allegations" or "*mere* allegations", the latter alone is to be decided by the arbitral tribunal; *serious* allegations of fraud (according to this decision) are not arbitrable;[29]

(viii) eviction or tenancy matters governed by special statutes where the tenant enjoys statutory protection against eviction and only the special courts are conferred jurisdiction to order eviction or to decide disputes between landlord or tenant.[30]

(ix) *excepted matters* are not arbitrable: once the parties have decided that certain matters are to be determined by (say), the superintending engineer and it is also mentioned that his decision would be final the same cannot be the subject matter of arbitration: *M/s. Mitra Guha Builders (India) Co.,* vs. *Oil and Natural Gas Corporation Ltd.*, a Bench decision of 3 judges of the Supreme Court reported in 2019 (15) SCALE 501.

Re(v) *There have been far too many amendments to the 1996 Act—resulting in some confusion and inconsistencies in the law.*

For instance, although Section 11(1) even after the amendment of 2019 continues to provide that "a person of any nationality may be an arbitrator" qualifications for an arbitrator in an arbitration under Part-I are now prescribed under Section 43J read with the Eighth Schedule ("a person shall not be qualified to be an arbitrator unless he is an advocate within the meaning of the Advocates Act, 1961.....") or fulfils the requirements mentioned in sub-clauses (ii) to (ix) of the Eighth Schedule.

End Notes:

1. Subject to an amendment introduced as a proviso to Section 2(2) by Amending Act 3 of 2016 reading as follows:

   This Part, (Part-I) shall apply where the place of arbitration is in India: [Provided that subject to an agreement to the contrary, the provisions of Sections 9, 27 and Clause (a) of sub-section (1) and sub-section (3) of Section 37 shall also apply to international commercial arbitration, even if the place of arbitration is outside India, and an arbitral award made or to be made in such place is enforceable and recognised under the provisions of Part II of this Act].

2. "Foreign Awards" given or made after the commencement of the Arbitration and Conciliation Act, 1996, i.e. from 22 August 1996, have been held to be governed by the 1996 Act, although the proceedings for arbitration had commenced (with place of arbitration in India) prior to the coming into force of the 1996 Act.
3. Judges in England as well (after enactment of the English Arbitration Act 1996) had cautioned against the use of English decisions before its enactment. In *Seabridge* vs. *Shipping A. B.* vs. *Orssleff's* (1999) 2 L.L.R. 685 at page 690; it was stated: "International users of London arbitration should, in my view, be able to rely on the clear 'user-friendly language' of the Act and should not have to be put to the trouble or an expense of having regard to the pre-1996 Act, law on issues where the provisions of the Act set out the law".
4. *Sundaram Finance* vs. *NEPC India Ltd.* 1999 (2) SCC 479 at page 483 (2 judges); followed in firm *Ashok Traders* vs. *Gurumukh Das Saluja* 2004 (3) SCC 155 at para-13 pages 165-166 the court held that: *"The A & C Act, 1996 is a long leap in the direction of alternate dispute resolution systems. It is based on the UNCITRAL Model.* The decided cases under the preceding Act of 1940 have to be applied with caution for determining the issues arising for decision under the new Act." Similar observations were made in: *Rashtriya Ispat Nigam Ltd.* vs. *Verma Transport Co.* 2006 (7) SCC 275, 282 para 9, 10 page-282; also see: *Pandey and Co. Builders Pvt. Ltd* vs. *State of Bihar* 2007 (1) SCC 467, 470, 471, paras 11 and 13; and

in *India Household and Healthcare Ltd.* vs. *LG Household and Healthcare Ltd.* 2007 (5) SCC 510 para-9 page 515

5. Subject to a subsequent amendment to Section 2(2) a Proviso was introduced to Section 2(2) by Amending Act 3 of 2016 reading as follows:

   "(2) This Part shall apply where the place of arbitration is in India:

   "[Provided that subject to an agreement to the contrary, the provisions of Sections 9, 27 and Clause (a) of sub-section (1) and sub-section (3) of Section 37 shall also apply to international commercial arbitration, even if the place of arbitration is outside India, and an arbitral award made or to be made in such place is enforceable and recognised under the provisions of Part II of this Act]."

6. (2002) 4 SCC 105 (Bench of 3 judges)
7. Article 8: Arbitration agreement and arbitration claim before the court.

   Article 9: Arbitration agreement and interim measures by the court.

   Article 35: Recognition and enforcement (of awards).

   Article 36: Grounds for refusing recognition or enforcement (of awards).
8. (2012) 9 SCC 552
9. In paragraph 10.27 at page 578.
10. The Arbitration and Conciliation Act, 1996 stands amended with effect from 23 October 2015, by several amendments made by Parliament in the Arbitration and Conciliation (Amendment) Act, 2015 (Act 3 of 2016). Although in the case of a foreign award *Bhatia* had applied the provisions of Section 9 (Interim Measures by Court) (and that decision stands overruled by *Bharat Aluminium*

Co. (*Balco*), 2012, the Arbitration and Conciliation (amendment) Act, 2015 (Act 3 of 2016) now expressly provides inter alia that interim measures of protection set out in Section 9 in Part-I, also apply to "international commercial arbitration" even when the place of arbitration is outside India and even when the arbitration award made or to be made is enforceable and recognised under the provisions of Part-II of the 1996 Act.

11. (2015)10 SCC 213
12. Section 5: "Notwithstanding anything contained in any other law for the time being in force, in matters governed by this part, no judicial authority shall intervene except where so provided in this part."
13. Article 5 (Extent of Court Intervention): "In matters governed by this law, no court shall intervene except where so provided in this law."
14. *P. Anand Gajapathi Raju* vs. *P. V. G. Raju* 2000 (4) SCC 539, 541.
15. See *SBP* vs. *Patel Engineering Ltd.*—2005 (8) SCC 618 paragraph 19 of the majority judgment (p. 649): "a judicial authority as such is not defined in the Act it would certainly include the "Court" as defined in Sec. 2(e) of the Act and would also in our opinion include other courts and may even include a special tribunal like the consumer forum".
16. I.A. No. 6663/2003 in Suit No. 1268/2003 (Delhi High Court, Judgment dated 5 May 2004) (reported only in http://indiankanoon.org/doc/1826182)
17. See AIR 2014 S.C. 968 at page 975.
18. AIR 2014 S.C. 968 at 975-976.
19. 2011 Bombay C.R. Suppl. Page 4 (overruled in AIR 2014 S.C. 968)
20. AIR 2014 SC 968 at 982
21. In contrast to the UK where the trend is towards expanding the range of disputes that are capable of being submitted

to arbitration—See David St. Sutton, Judith Gill, Mathew Gearing: Editors of Russell on *Arbitration*, 24th Edition, Sweet & Maxwell, USA, 2015, Pp. 71 to 76. It is stated in paragraph 2.080 that there is no agreed definition of arbitratbility and none is provided in the English Arbitration Act. The Act only recognises the right of the courts to refuse recognition or enforcement of an award that is in respect of a matter which is not capable of settlement by arbitration (page 71), but the heads on limits of arbitrability (in the UK) have been set out at pages 71 to 73.

Very recently UNCITRAL proposed a solution to reach a consensus on a list of non-arbitrable issues (A/C N. 9/460 paragraph 33). This has been adopted by the German Arbitration Law 1998 (Section 1030) as well as by the Tunisian Arbitration Code 1993 (Article 7) reproduced at page 40 of Dr Peter Binder's 2019 publication of his Fourth Edition of *International Commercial Arbitration and Mediation in UNCITRAL Model Law Jurisdictions*, published by Wolters Kluwer, Netherlands. (The book was registered in the US Library of Congress only in the second half of 2019.)

22. *Booz Allen and Hamilton Inc* vs. *SBI House Finance Ltd.*—2011 (5) SCC 532 paragraph 36; Followed in *M.S.P. Infrastructure Ltd.* vs. *Madhya Pradesh Road Development Corporation*, 2015 (13) SCC 713, 720; *A. Ayyasamy* vs. *A. Paramasivam*, (2016) 10 SCC 386; *Rakesh Malhotra* vs. *Rajinder Kumar Malhotra*, (2015) 127 CLA 140 (Bom); *Eros International Media Ltd.* vs. *Telemax Links India Private Limited*, 2016 SCC Online Bom 2179; *The Indian Performing Society* vs. *Entertainment Network (India) Ltd.* 2016 SCC Online Bom 5893; *Vimal Kishor Shah* vs. *Jayesh Dinesh Shah*, (2016) 8 SCC 788, *Sumana Mol P.S.* vs. *Bharath Sanchar Nigam*, 2016 SCC Online Kerala 35063; *Sujith P.P.* vs. *Bharath Sanchar Nigam Ltd.*, 2016 SCC Online Kerala 33519; *P. Ponnoppan* vs. *Bharath Sanchar*

Nigam Ltd. 2016 SCC Online Kerala 33518; *Ranjit Kumar Bose* vs. *Anannya Chowdhury*, 2014 (11) SCC 446; *Smt. Penumalli Sulochana* vs. *Harish Rawtani*, 2013 (4) Arb LR 264 (Andhra Pradesh)."

23. *A. Ayyasamy* vs. *A. Paramasivam & Others* 2016(10) SCC 386, 403, 409 (Fraud); *Abdul Kadir S. Bubere* vs. *Madhav Oak*—AIR 1962 S.C. 406; *N. Radhakrishnan* vs. *Maestro Engineer*—2010 (1) SCC 72; *Narasmicha Raju* vs. *Gurumurthy Raju*—AIR 1963 S.C. 607
24. *Malka* vs. *Sardar*—AIR 1929 Lahore 394
25. *Mahadeo Prasad* vs. *Biswanath Prasad*—ILR 30 Allahabad 137; *Sami Chetty* vs. *Adai Kalam Chetty*—AIR 1924 Madras 484
26. *Ladha Singh* vs. *Bhag Singh*—34 IC 549
27. *Mommohini* vs. *Dayachand* ILR 31 Cal. 357; *Khela* vs. *Chet Ra.* AIR 1952 Punjab 67; (Question of genuineness of a Will). But See *Charanjilal Shrilal* vs. *Jasjit Singh*—1993 (2) SCC 507 paragraph 18, 20, "Construction of a Will can be Arbitrated."
28. See *Emaar MGF Land Limited* vs. *Aftab Singh*: a recent decision of a Bench of 2 judges of the Supreme Court of India (10 December 2018) holding that the remedy provided by the Arbitration Act 1996 is barred by implication. However, it was also clarified that where a person entitled to seek an additional special remedy provided by the statute (the Consumer Protection Act) does not opt for the additional special remedy, and is a party to an arbitration agreement there is no prohibition for disputes being proceeded with in arbitration.
29. *A. Ayyasamy* vs. *P. Paramasivam* 2016 (10) SCC 386, paras 17, 18, 22, 23, 24; Also see: *Ameetalchand* vs. *Rishabh Enterprises*, (2018)15 SCC 678: but these decisions are contrary to the law declared earlier: e.g. the case of *World Sport Group Mauritius Ltd.* AIR 2014 S.C. 968, page 975.
30. In *Himangi Enterprises* vs. *Kamaljeet Singh Ahluwalia*, 2017 (10) SCC 706 (2 judges) it was held that matters relating to

tenancy or leave-and-licence agreements were not arbitrable. (See also two earlier decisions— *Vishwanath Sood* vs. *Union of India*—1989 (1) SCC 657; and Prabartak Commercial Corpn. vs. Chief Administrator—1991 (1) SCC 498.

The correctness of the decision in *Himangni Enterprises* (2017) has been questioned in a later case reported in 2019 2 Arb.L.R. 121 (SC). In the last-mentioned case (*Vidya Drolia* vs. *Durga Trading Corporation* 2019, it has been stated that the decision of the Bench of two judges in *Himangi Enterprises* that the mere fact that an exemption from the Rent Act is available cannot mean that the matter becomes non arbitrable. *Vidya Drolia* was a case under the Transfer of Property Act, 1882, an Act silent on arbitrability; and court said that the judgment in *Himangi Enterpeises* will "require a relook by a bench of three Hon'ble Judges of this Court".

4

Analysis and Comments

Subsequent Amendments

The Arbitration and Conciliation Act 1996 states up front in its Preamble:

> "WHEREAS the United Nations Commission on International Trade Law (UNCITRAL) has adopted the UNCITRAL Model Law on International Commercial Arbitration in 1985;
>
> AND WHEREAS the General Assembly of the United Nations has recommended that all countries give due consideration to the said Model Law, in view of the desirability of uniformity of the law of arbitral procedures and the specific needs of international commercial arbitration practice;
>
> AND WHEREAS the UNCITRAL has adopted the UNCITRAL Conciliation Rules in 1980;
>
> AND WHEREAS the General Assembly of the United Nations has recommended the use of the said Rules in cases where a dispute arises in the context of international commercial relations and the parties seek an amicable settlement of that dispute by recourse to conciliation;
>
> AND WHEREAS the said Model Law and Rules make significant contribution to the establishment of a unified

legal framework for the fair and efficient settlement of disputes arising in international commercial relations;

AND WHEREAS it is expedient to make law respecting arbitration and conciliation, taking into account the aforesaid Model Law and Rules;

BE it enacted by Parliament in the Forty-seventh Year of the Republic of India as follows . . ."

And by Section 85, all prior enactments relating to arbitration—The Arbitration Protocol and Convention Act 1937, The Arbitration Act 1940 and the Foreign Awards Recognition and Enforcement Act 1961—have been repealed.

***

The Arbitration and Conciliation Act of 1996 (with the alterations and additions effected by Amending Act 3 of 2016 (as well the subsequent Amendment Act No. 33 of 2019) extends to the whole of India. It is divided into three parts (and a fourth):

"Part-I: (ARBITRATION)
(along with the newly-added Part-1A—
(ARBITRATION COUNCIL OF INDIA and Arbitration Centre)

Part-II:
Enforcement of Certain Foreign Awards
Chapter I: (NEW YORK CONVENTION AWARDS); and

Chapter II: GENEVA CONVENTION AWARDS

Part-III:
Conciliation.

Part-IV:
Suplementary Provisions."

Each of the first three "Supplementary Provisions" are virtually separate enactments.

In *Fuerst Day Lawson* vs. *Jindal Export* (2011) 8 SCC 333 (para 56), the Supreme Court said that: "a mere glance at the 1996 Act (that is as it was enacted) is sufficient to show that under its scheme the provisions relating to the three enactments (Part-I, Part-II and Part-III) are kept separately from each other."[1]

***

Part-I: ARBITRATION

Sections 2 to 43, in Part-I, substantially correspond (though not exactly) to Chapters I to VIII of the UNCITRAL Model Law 1985[2] *sometimes with additions, at other times with deletions, but conforming generally to the pattern of the UNCITRAL Model Law, 1985.*

Part-I consists of Chapters I to X which follow closely the provisions of the UNCITRAL Model Law on International Commercial Arbitration 1985.[3] The General Assembly of the UN whilst approving the Model Law on International Commercial Arbitration that had been prepared by the

United Nations Commission on International Trade Law (UNCITRAL) had expressly recommended (by Resolution dated 4 December 1985) that:

> "All states give due consideration to the said Model Law on International Commercial Arbitration in view of the desirability of uniformity of the law of arbitral procedures and the specific needs of international commercial arbitration practice."

The Resolution adopted by consensus, was the culmination of a universal project to draft a model law on arbitration designed for use in legal and political systems in developed as well as developing countries and in all geographic regions.

The most important provision in Part-I of the 1996 Act is its *Scope*—defined in Section 2(2):

> "(2) *This Part shall apply where the place of arbitration is in India.*
> (Provided that subject to an agreement to the contrary, the provisions of sections 9, 27 and clause [b] of sub-section (1) and sub-section (3) of section 37 shall also apply to international commercial arbitration, even if the place of arbitration is outside India, and an arbitral award made or to be made in such place is enforceable and recognised under the provisions of Part II of this Act)"[4]. [Proviso added by amending Act 3 of 2016].

The rules applicable to the substance of dispute (for the arbitration under Part-I which is to be at a place in India) are set out in Section 28(1) which commences with the words:

"Where the place of arbitration is situated in India

(a) in an arbitration other than an international commercial arbitration . . .
(b) in international commercial arbitration . . ."

Because of stray remarks in a "*judgment*" reported of a single judge of the Supreme Court of India in *TDM Infrastructure Pvt. Ltd.* vs. *UE Development India Pvt. Ltd.*[5] a belief was entertained that having regard to Section 2(2) and Section 28 of the 1996 Act, two Indian parties (individuals, firms or entirely Indian companies) must at all times not only have their place of arbitration in India, but their commercial agreement must also be governed by Indian law. The stray remarks[6] were made not whilst sitting in a Bench as always required by the Supreme Court Rules[7] but when pronouncing an order (appointing an Arbitrator) under Section 11 of the 1996 Act: the order being passed as delegate of the Chief Justice of India.

No part of the 1996 Act (neither in Part-I, nor in Part-II, or in Part-III, or Part-IV) prohibits parties from agreeing (in a commercial agreement) that when disputes arise the place of arbitration should be a place outside India or that such an arbitration must also be governed as between the parties only by Indian law. The observations of Justice S. B. Sinha (in the *TDM* Case) that it is contrary to "public policy" for two Indian parties to agree to go to arbitration and be governed by some non-Indian law, is not supported either by any provision in the Contract Act 1872, nor by any provisions of the Arbitration and Conciliation Act, 1996—as enacted or as amended. The remarks are not even *obiter* because in a later judgment of the Supreme Court of India it has been held that an order of a single judge—as delegate of the Chief Justice of India under Section 11 of the 1996 Act—"has no precedential value"[8].

In the now celebrated *Bharat Aluminium Co.* (*Balco*) case (2012)[9]—a decision of a Bench of 5 judges—the Supreme Court of India with reference to the *TDM* case (2008 (14) SCC 271) expressly rejected the argument of the counsel that Section 28 of the 1996 Act "was not confined to arbitration which took place in India." Referring to Section 28 of 1996 Act the Court, in *Bharat Aluminium Co.* (*Balco*), said in paragraph 118:

> "...to suit India, conflict of law rules have been suitably modified, where the arbitration is in India. *This will not apply where the seat is outside India. In that event, the conflict of laws rules of the country in which the arbitration takes place would have to be applied.* Therefore, in our opinion, the emphasis placed on the expression "where the place of arbitration is situated in India", by the learned senior counsel for the appellants, is not indicative of the fact that the intention of Parliament was to give an extra-territorial operation to Part-I of the Arbitration Act, 1996." (Emphasis supplied)

In another paragraph of the judgment (with reference to the *TDM Infrastructure Case*) the Supreme Court (in *Bharat Aluminium Co.*) specifically made mention of the fact that this case was under Section 11 (*Appointment of an Arbitrator by the Chief Justice of India or a judge of the Supreme Court acting as a delegate*).

In a later decision of the Supreme Court of India in the case of *Sasan Power Ltd.* vs. *North American Coal Corporation India Pvt. Ltd.* (2016)[10] the question whether two Indian parties could provide in their agreement that dispute could be decided at a place abroad according to a law of the choice of the parties was avoided. However, the High Court of Madhya Pradesh (where the *Sasan* case[11] had originated) in its judgment had expressly disapproved the remarks of Justice S. B. Sinha in the *TDM* case holding that:

> "Therefore, it is clear that based on the seat of arbitration the question of permitting two Indian companies/ parties to arbitrate out of India is permissible."

In that *case* (*Sasan Power case)* there was in fact an express contractual stipulation that not only would the place of arbitration be in London but, in addition, the governing law of the agreement would be the law of the United Kingdom (not the law of India). But, when the *Sasan* case reached the Supreme Court of India (under Article 136 of the Constitution of India) and the ultimate decision of the Madhya Pradesh High Court was upheld, the Supreme Court (a Bench decision of 2 judges) stated—erroneously—(in para 28 of its judgment[12]) that "*the question whether two Indian companies could enter into agreements to be governed by the laws of another country would not arise in this case*". In fact, it did arise in the case and was so decided by the Division Bench of the High Court of Madhya Pradesh[13] (without any subsequent dissent in the Supreme Court).

There is no prohibition for two Indian parties entering into a commercial agreement for arbitration of their disputes at a place outside India or for disputes being decided according to a law of their choice. Section 28(1) of the 1996 Act, ("*Rules applicable to substance of dispute*") begins with the premise "*where the place of arbitration is situated in India*"—and controls the entirety of what follows in Section 28 (1).

Conclusion: No part of the 1996 Act (neither in Part-I, Part-II, Part-III or Part-IV) prohibits parties in India from contracting that their disputes be referred to arbitration to a place outside India, nor does any part of the 1996 Act (nor any provision of the Contract Act, 1872) prohibit Indian parties from having their disputes arbitrated at a place *overseas* or according to a law that is not Indian law.

***

Chapter-I: General Provisions—Sections 2 to 6

Section 2 incorporates definitions occurring in the Act, including (for the first time) a definition of "International Commercial Arbitration" (that adopts, only in part, the definition recommended in Article 1(3) of the Model Law). The 1996 Act defines "international commercial arbitration" only for purposes of Part-I (i.e. where the place of arbitration is in India) and the definition reads as follows:

> "*International Commercial Arbitration* means an arbitration relating to disputes arising out of legal relationships, whether contractual or not, considered as commercial under the law in force in India and where at least one of the parties is:

(i) an individual who is a national of, or habitually resident in, any country other than India; or
(ii) a body corporate which is incorporated in any country other than India; or
(iii) an association or a body of individuals whose central management and control is exercised in any country other than India; or
(iv) the Government of a foreign country."[14]

Under the recommendatory definition in the Model Law "international commercial arbitration" also includes (Clause 3[c]) "an arbitration where parties have expressly agreed that the subject-matter of the agreement relates to more than one country" but this has not been adopted in the 1996 Act. This clause in the Model Law extending the definition to the volition of parties is not part of "international commercial arbitration" as defined in the 1996 Act.

Some of the decisions of the Supreme Court of India handed down so far pertaining to "International Commercial Arbitration" (as now defined in the 1996 Act) are set out below:

(i) *Enercon (India) Ltd. and Ors.* vs. *Enercon GMBH and Ors.* (14 February 2014)*: AIR 2014 SC 3152*
(ii) *Duro Felguera S.A.* vs. *Gangavaram Port Limited* (10 October 2017): *AIR 2017 SC 5070 = 2017(6) Arb LR 1 (SC)*
(iii) *Union of India (UOI)* vs. *Hardy Exploration and Production (India) Inc. (25 September 2018): AIR 2018 SC 4871: (*Determining that (juridical) *seat* of

arbitration may be different from *venue*): However, the decision in *Hardy Exploration and Production (India) Inc* (determining that judicial *seat* of arbitration may be different from *venue*) has been questioned by a later bench of the court (also of 3 judges) 10 December 2019: in *BGS SGS Soma JV.* vs. *NHPC Ltd.* reported in 2019(17) SCALE 369 at pages 413-419 where it was held that the judgment in *Hardy Exploration and Production India Ltd.*, being contrary to a Bench decision of five judges in *BALCO* (2012) "cannot be considered to be good law".

(iv) *Vedanta Ltd.* vs. *Shenzen Shandong Nuclear Power Construction Co. Ltd.* (*11 October 2018*): *AIR 2018 SC 4773 = 2018* (*6*) *Arb LR 163 (SC)*

(v) *Ssangyong Engineering & Construction Co. Ltd. vs. National Highways Authority of India* (*NHAI*): *2019* (*3*) *Arb L R 152(SC) 2019 (8) SCALE page 41* (*S.C.*).

***

Chapter-II: Arbitration Agreement—Sections 7 to 9

Article 7 of the Model Law (*Definition and Form of Arbitration Agreement*)

It defines "Arbitration Agreement" and provides that it has to be in writing. It had been held long ago by the High Court of Hong Kong (in June 1994), in a case reported in (1994), Vol. 1, Hong Kong Cases 734, that an agreement to arbitrate contained in Articles of Association of a Company (incorporated in Hong Kong) was a valid arbitration agreement under the Model Law. It was held that Article 7 created a binding agreement between the company and its members.

Section 7 of the 1996 Act, corresponds to Article 7 of the Model Law.

In *Tamil Nadu Electricity Board* vs. *Sumathi* 2000 (4) SCC 543, it was held (on the facts of that case) that there was no arbitration agreement within the meaning of Section 7 of the 1996 Act; and in *Jagdish Chander* vs. *Ramesh Chander* 2007 (5) SCC 719 it was stated that: "the existence of an arbitration agreement as defined is a condition precedent for exercise of power to appoint an arbitrator/tribunal under Section 11 of the Act", i.e. appointment by the chief justice of the high court or by his delegate: a judge of the court. To the same effect are the decisions in *Maharishi Dayanand University* vs. *Anand Cooperative Society Ltd.*: 2007 (5) SCC 295; and in *Shakti Bhog Foods Ltd.* vs. *Kola Shipping Ltd.* 2009 (2) SCC 134. It has been held by the Supreme Court of India that the validity of an arbitration agreement does not depend upon the number of arbitrators specified[15].

Under the Indian law a two-tier arbitration is not prohibited. Parties may choose to agree (under Section 7), to a second or an appellate arbitration (even in London) in accordance with Rules of Conciliation and Arbitration of the International Chamber of Commerce (ICC), Paris. Such an arbitration clause in the agreement between the parties does not violate any fundamental law or public policy: it was so held in *M/s. Centrotrade Minerals Inc.* vs. *Hindustan Copper Ltd.* —AIR 2017 SC 185 (3J).

The definition of "arbitration agreement" has been extended by Court decisions to non-signatories e.g. groups of companies where the companies together constitute a single economic entity. It was first involed by the Supreme Court of India in *Chloro Controls India Pvt. Ltd. vs. Severn Trent Water Purification Inc.*: 2013 (1) SCC 641 (in the case of an International Commercial Agreement); later in *SEI Adhavan Power Pvt. Ltd. vs. Jinneng Clean Energy Technology Ltd.*, 2018 (4) CTC 46 (Madras) (with respect to a foreign seated arbitration); and later again in *Ameet Lal Chand Shah vs. Rishabh Enterprises* 2018 (15) SCC 678 (in the case of a domestic arbitration); the most recent decision is the case of *Mahanagar Telephone Nigam Ltd. vs. Canara Bank* 2019 (10) scale 619 (Supreme Court of India Judgment dated 8.8.2019).

***

Article 8 of the Model Law (Arbitration Agreement and Substantive Claim before Court)

(Corresponds to Article II(3) of the New York Convention, 1958) It provides that "unless it finds that the Agreement is null and void, inoperative or incapable of being performed" a court before which an action is brought in a matter which is the subject of an arbitration agreement *shall*, refer parties to arbitration if a party so requests not later than when submitting its first statement on the substance of the dispute. Article 8 of the Model law requires a court to recognise and give effect to an arbitration agreement and provides for a critical element of arbitral law: viz. the exclusive competence of the arbitral tribunal to decide the substance of the dispute that is the subject of a valid arbitration agreement. The scope of the court's inquiry under the Model Law into the validity of the arbitration agreement is the same as under Article II(3) of the New York Convention.[16] In Canada it has been held by the Federal Court that a court may stay a proceeding under Article 8 in an action involving non-parties to an arbitration clause so as to avoid fragmented litigation and potentially conflicting results.[17]

Section 8 of the 1996 Act, as enacted was a replica of Article 8 of the Model Law. But an entirely new Section 8 has been substituted by the Amending Act No. 3 of 2016 (w.e.f. October 2015) where the emphasis is not on the end—words occurring in Article 8 as initially enacted (viz. "unless it finds that the agreement is null and void, inoperative or incapable of being performed"). These words have been now substituted by a new set of words: "unless it finds that prima facie no valid arbitration agreement exists".

In India it has been held that the termination of an agreement by mutual consent does not render the arbitration clause inoperative—reference of disputes to arbitration being mandatory: *Hema Khattar* vs. *Shiv Khera*: AIR 2017 SC 1793 is a decision under Section 8 *as amended* and it refers to an earlier decision reported in *P. Anand Gajapathi Raju* vs. *P.V.G. Raju*: AIR 2000 SC 1886 = (2000) 4 SCC 539 at a time when Section 8, as enacted, was in force. In *Kalpna Kothari* vs. *Sadhna Yadav* reported in AIR 2001

SC 404) it was pointed out by the Supreme Court that the scope and object of Section 8 (as first enacted) was entirely different from Section 34 of the Arbitration Act, 1940, which had left it to the discretion of the court whether or not to stay a suit on a contract containing an arbitration clause. The ratio would apply equally to Section 8 as now amended.

***

Article 9 of the Model Law (Arbitration Agreement and Interim Measures by Court)

It codifies the dual principle that a party does not waive its right to go to arbitration by requesting or obtaining interim measures of protection from a national court, and that a national court is not prevented from granting such measures merely by reason of the existence of an arbitration agreement. The need for a provision like Article 9 arose out of the experience (of some members of the Working Group) of reported decisions under the New York Convention which had reached divergent conclusions on whether they could or could not grant requests for attachments and other interim measures in matters governed by arbitration agreements. *Article 9 therefore established that interim measures by a national court were and are compatible with arbitration.* Article 9 has been broadly construed, for instance, it includes a request to a court to compel a third party to give evidence which could be recorded at the arbitration. See *Delphi Petroleum Ltd.* vs. *Derin Shipping Federal Court of Canada* (1 December 1993) reported in 1993 73 FTR 241 CLOUT—*(Case*

Law on Uncitral Texts): a legal database of worldwide court decisions and arbitral awards on UNCITRAL texts.

Section 9 of the 1996 Act, which provides for interim measures by the courts and prescribes a time-frame, goes further than the Article. It sets out in detail the interim measures. Section 9 states that a party may, before or during arbitral proceedings or at any time after the making of the arbitral award (but before it is enforced in accordance with Section 36), apply to a court either for the appointment of a guardian for a minor or for an interim measure of protection in respect of the preservation, interim custody or sale of any goods which are the subject-matter of the arbitration agreement, or securing the amount in dispute in the arbitration, or the detention, preservation or inspection of any property or thing which is the subject-matter of the dispute in arbitration, or for an interim injunction or the appointment of a receiver, or (finally) for such other interim measure of protection as may appear to the arbitral tribunal to be just and convenient, it being additionally provided that a court, under Section 9, has the same power for making orders, as it has for the purpose of, and in relation to, any proceedings before it.

Reported decisions of the Supreme Court of India on Section 9 include:

(1) *Firm Ashok Traders and Ors.* vs. *Gurumukh Das Saluja and Ors.* 2004 (3) SCC 155 (locus standi for filing application under Section 9);

(2) *National Aluminium Co. Ltd.* vs. *Gerald Metals SA*, 2004 (9) SCC 307 (a case under Section 9(ii)(d)

—for interim injunction or for the appointment of receiver);

(3) *Arvind Constructions Co. Pvt. Ltd.* vs. *Kalinga Mining Corporation and Ors.* 2007 (6) SCC 798 (which lays down that the general rule that governs a court considering whether or not to grant an interim injunction at the threshold, applies also to applications under Section 9); and

(4) *B.E. Simoes Von Staraburg Niedenthal* vs. *Chhattisgarh Investment Ltd.*, 2015 (12) SCC 225 where it has been held that where a particular court only has exclusive jurisdiction, an order under Section 9 cannot be passed by a court elsewhere.

Section 9(2) and (3) of the 1996 Act are not part of the UNCITRAL Model Law. These sub-clauses of Section 9 have been added by the Amending Act 3 of 2016 (w.e.f. October 2015). They provide that where a court passes an order for any interim measure of protection under Section 9(1), the arbitration proceedings must be commenced within a period of 90 days from the date of such orders (or within such further time as the court may permit). They also provide that once the Arbitration Tribunal has been constituted, the court ought not to entertain an application for interim measures, unless the court finds that circumstances exist which may not otherwise render *efficacious* the remedy provided for under Section 17 ("Interim Measures ordered by the Arbitral Tribunal").

***

Chapter-III: Composition of Arbitral Tribunal—Sections 10 to 15

Articles 10 *to* 15 *of the Model Law* provide for the composition of the arbitral tribunal—Number of arbitrators (Article 10); Appointment of arbitrators (Article 11); Grounds for Challenge (Article 12), only if circumstances exist that give rise to justifiable doubts as to impartiality or independence, or lack of qualifications of the arbitrator. Challenge Procedure—Article 13; Failure or impossibility to act—Article 14: i.e. consequences where an arbitrator becomes *de jure* or *de facto* unable to perform his functions or for other reasons fails to act without undue delay; and finally Article 15 provides for appointment of a substitute arbitrator where the mandate of an arbitrator terminates under article 13 or 14 or because of his withdrawal from office for any other reason, a substitute arbitrator has then to be appointed (according to the rules that are applicable to appointment of an arbitrator in replacement of one that had been initially appointed).

Sections 10 *to* 15 of the 1996 Act provide for the composition of the arbitral tribunal and for the number of arbitrators (Section 10); Appointment of arbitrators where parties fail to agree on the arbitrator (Section 11)[18]; Grounds for challenge (Section 12); Challenge procedure (Section 13); Failure or impossibility to act (Section 14); and termination of mandate and substitution of arbitrators (Section 15).

Section 10 of the Act (Number of arbitrators) was expected to conform to Article 10 of the Model Law, but was drafted differently, which resulted in a contention being raised which, if accepted, might have rendered the 1996 Act unworkable. Fortunately, a pragmatic and statesman-like decision of the Supreme Court of India prevented it.[19]

***

Article 11 of the Model Law provides procedure for the appointment of arbitrators. Under it, there are essentially three methods to secure the appointment of an arbitrator:

First, the Article establishes the basic principle that the parties may agree on a procedure for appointing arbitrators and that the chosen procedure will be recognised and not supplemented by the courts.

Second, if the parties do not reach such an agreement, Article 11 provides a mechanism for appointing either a three-person tribunal or a one-person arbitral tribunal without the involvement of the courts.

Third, if all else fails, that is, if the procedure agreed on by the parties or the procedure set forth in the law fails to produce the necessary appointment, Article 11 directs the "court" (the "other authority" specified in Article 6 of the Model Law[20]) to appoint the arbitrator or arbitrators and provides guidelines for the court to follow with respect to independence, impartiality, and nationality.

Section 11 as enacted in the 1996 Act, (and as amended by Act 3 of 2016), had made a departure from Article

11 of the Model Law, as it now stands (after the further amendments of 2019), there is yet another departure from the Model Law.

Section 11 (as enacted and as amended by Act 3 of 2016) had provided that a person of any nationality may be appointed an arbitrator unless otherwise agreed by the parties, and also that parties were free to agree on a procedure for appointment of an arbitrator or arbitrators; and that failing agreement, or where a party failed to appoint an arbitrator, as was required under the agreed procedure, or the appointed arbitrators failed to reach an agreement expected of them under the procedure, or if a person (or an institution) failed to perform the functions entrusted to them under that procedure, a party may request the Supreme Court or a High Court to take the necessary steps for appointment of arbitrator(s).

Provision was also made that where a party failed to appoint an arbitrator within the stipulated time, or where two appointed arbitrators failed to agree on a third arbitrator being appointed within a stipulated time, the appointment must be made upon request of a party by the Chief Justice of the Supreme Court of India (or his delegate—a judge of that court) in the case of an "International Commercial Arbitration"; and in all other cases, by the Chief Justice of the High Court concerned (or his delegate—(a judge of that court)[21].

In *Konkan Railway Corporation Ltd. and Ors.* vs. *Rani Construction Pvt. Ltd.* 2002 (2) SCC 388 in a Bench decision of 5 judges of the Supreme Court of India, it was held that Section 11 (as it was worded after Amending Act

3 of 2016) could not be interpreted on the basis of Article 11 of the UNCITRAL Model Law, since the provision made (in the 1996 Act) for the chief justice or any person or institution designated by him, to make appointment of arbitrators was unique, and not envisaged in the Model Law. In a later decision, *State of West Bengal and Others* vs. *Associated Contractors* 2015 (1) SCC 32, a Bench of 3 judges had also held that anything said by a delegate of the chief justice (either of the Supreme Court of India or of a High Court) under Section 11, was not to be regarded as said by a "Court" as defined in the 1996 Act. And also that, the ruling/decision of a chief justice or his delegate under Section 11, (even though reported in the law reports), was not a "decision" of the Supreme Court, and had no precedential value.

In a case other than that of an "international commercial arbitration", provision had been also made in the law for the fees of the arbitral tribunal. They were to be in accordance with provisions made in the Fourth Schedule to the 1996 Act as enacted: varying according to the sums in dispute.

However, the system of appointment of arbitrators as had been prescribed in Section 11 of the 1996 Act, as enacted, and as amended by Act 3 of 2016, now stands altered after the amendment of July 2019. *Section 11* as now further amended by Amending Act No. 33 of 2019 (The Arbitration and Conciliation (Amendment) Act 2019, reads as follows[22] but the provision will become applicable only after July 2019):

Appointment of Arbitrators (set out in extenso is now worded as follows):

(1) A person of any nationality may be an arbitrator, unless otherwise agreed by the parties.

(2) Subject to sub-section (6), the parties are free to agree on a procedure for appointing the arbitrator or arbitrators.

(3) Failing any agreement referred to in sub-section (2), in an arbitration with three arbitrators, each party shall appoint one arbitrator, and the two appointed arbitrators shall appoint the third arbitrator who shall act as the presiding arbitrator.

(3A) The Supreme Court and the high court shall have the power to designate, arbitral institutions, from time to time, which have been graded by the Council under Section 43-I, (in Part-1A) for the purposes of this Act:

Provided that in respect of those high court jurisdictions, where no graded arbitral institutions are available, then, the Chief Justice of the concerned high court may maintain a panel of arbitrators for discharging the functions and duties of arbitral institution and any reference to the arbitrator shall be deemed to be an arbitral institution for the purposes of this section and the arbitrator appointed by a party shall be entitled to such fee at the rate as specified in the Fourth Schedule:

Provided further, that the Chief Justice of the concerned high court may, from time to time, review the panel of arbitrators."

(4) If the appointment procedure in sub-section (3) applies and

A party fails to appoint an arbitrator within 30 days from the receipt of a request to do so from the other party; or

If the two appointed arbitrators fail to agree on the third arbitrator within 30 days from the date of their appointment, the appointment shall be made on an application of the party by the arbitral institution designated by the Supreme Court in the case of International Commercial Arbitration or by the high court, in the case of arbitration other than International Commercial Arbitration, as the case may be.

(5) Failing any agreement referred to in sub-section (2) in an arbitration with a sole arbitrator if the parties fail to agree on the arbitrator within 30 days from receipt of a request by one party from the other party to so agree, the appointment shall be made on an application of the party by the arbitral institution, designated by the Supreme Court in the case of International Commercial Arbitration or by the high court, in the case of arbitration other

than International Commercial Arbitration, as the case may be.

(6) Where, under an appointment procedure agreed upon by the parties

(a) a party fails to act as required under that procedure; or
(b) the parties, or the two appointed arbitrators, fail to reach an agreement expected of them under that procedure; or
(c) a person, including an institution, fails to perform any function entrusted to him or it under that procedure

the appointment shall be made on an application by the arbitral institution designated by the Supreme Court in the case of International Commercial Arbitration or by the high court, in the case of an arbitration other than International Commercial Arbitration, as the case may be.

(6A) Sub-section (6A) in Section 11[23] (added by Amending Act 3 of 2016) has been omitted in 2019.

(6B) The designation of any person or institution by the Supreme Court or, as the case may be, the high court, for the purposes of this section shall not be regarded as a delegation of judicial power by the Supreme Court or the High Court.

(7) Sub-section (7) of section 11[24] as enacted is omitted in 2019.

(8) The arbitral institution referred to in sub-sections (4), (5) and (6) shall seek a disclosure in writing from the prospective arbitrator in terms of sub-section (1) of Section 12 and have due regard to

(a) any qualifications required for the arbitrator by the agreement of the parties; and
(b) the contents of the disclosure and other considerations as are likely to secure the appointment of an independent and impartial arbitrator.

(9) In the case of appointment of sole or third arbitrator in an International Commercial Arbitration the arbitral institution designated by the Supreme Court may appoint an arbitrator of a nationality other that the nationalities of the parties where the parties belong to different nationalities.

(10) Sub-section (10) of Section 11[25] has been also omitted in 2019.

(11) Where more than one request has been made under sub-section (4) or sub-section (5) or sub-section (6) to different arbitral institutions, the arbitral institution to which the request has been first made under the relevant sub-section shall be competent to appoint.

(12) Where the matter referred to in sub-sections (4), (5), (6) and (8) arise in an international commercial arbitration or any other arbitration, the reference to

the arbitral institution in those sub-sections shall be construed as a reference to the arbitral institution designated under sub-section (3A).

(13) An application made under this section for appointment of an arbitrator or arbitrators shall be disposed of by the arbitral institution within a period of thirty days from the date of service of notice on the opposite party.

(14) The arbitral institution shall determine the fees of the arbitral tribunal and the manner of its payment to the arbitral tribunal subject to the rates specified in the Fourth Schedule.

(Explanation: For the removal of doubts, it is hereby clarified that this sub-section shall not apply to international commercial arbitration and in arbitrations (other than international commercial arbitration) where parties have agreed for determination of fees as per the rules of an arbitral institution."[26])

Comment: Section 11(1) is now apparently inconsistent not only with Section 43J but also contrary to provisions now included in the Eighth Schedule.

***

Article 12 *of the Model Law* (*Grounds for challenge*)

The Working Group agreed at the outset on the central feature of this article—that it would not attempt to list in detail all possible connections to the parties or other circumstances that might justify a challenge[27]. The article provides two general formulae:

> *First*, an arbitrator may be challenged if circumstances exist that "give rise to justifiable doubts as to his impartiality or independence"
>
> *Second*, he (or she) may be challenged if the person does not possess qualifications agreed to by the parties.

The secretariat noted that national laws often list in detail all possible grounds for challenge. It also suggested that general tests like the ones ultimately included in Article 12 might be appropriate for a Model Law since they were likely to be more widely accepted than any single list of specific criteria.[28] The Working Group adopted this suggestion.

Section 12 *of the* 1996 *Act* (Grounds for challenge) was differently worded when enacted but was later substituted by a new section by Amendment Act No. 3 of 2016. It now follows the Model Law, but includes a provision that notwithstanding any prior agreement to the contrary, any person whose relationship with parties, counsel or subject-matter-of dispute falls under any of the categories specified in the (newly added) Seventh-Schedule will be ineligible to be appointed as an arbitrator.

***

Article 13 *of the Model Law* (*Challenge Procedure*)

It was agreed in the Working Group that the Model Law recognises freedom of parties to challenge an arbitrator on a wide variety of alternative considerations. The question that was left unresolved by Article 13, was the effect of a failure to raise a timely challenge. Neither the Working Group nor the Commission explicitly barred a party from raising a challenge during arbitral proceedings or subsequent court proceedings. It was however stressed that impartiality or independence of an arbitrator was mandatory, and parties could not agree to a partial or dependent arbitrator—since it was felt that a court would understandably hesitate to uphold an award issued by an arbitral tribunal constituted contrary to the mandatory requirements of the law particularly since it was felt by the Working Group that Article 34 of the Model Law appeared to allow an appeal against an arbitral award on the ground that the arbitrator was not impartial or independent.

Section 13 *of the* 1996 *Act*—The challenge procedure follows generally what is stated in Article 13 of the Model Law.

***

Article 14 *of the Model Law—Failure or Impossibility to Act.*

The grounds for termination of arbitration were taken from Article 13 of the UNCITRAL Arbitration Rules. If an arbitrator being de jure or de facto unable to perform this function, or for other reasons, fails to act without undue delay, his (or her) mandate terminates.

It was submitted that in judging whether an arbitrator failed to act the following consideration would be relevant. If he had done something and acted in a certain way, did his conduct fall clearly below the standard of what was reasonably expected from an arbitrator? Amongst the factors influencing the level of expectations were the ability to function efficiently and expeditiously and any special competence or other qualifications required of the arbitrator.

Article 14, as finally drafted, differed from Article 13(2) of the UNCITRAL Arbitration Rules in a major way—by the addition of the words "without undue delay" after the words "fails to act". As the Secretariat pointed out, there is in the Rules provision for an unstated time element, that is, the period of time during which the arbitrator should have acted but did not. The Commission decided to make this element explicit, partly in view of the fact that a great many national laws and arbitration rules contained provisions regarding speeding-up of arbitrations.

The Working Group however also decided not to place "a judge with-a-stop-watch "over the shoulder of every arbitrator and for that reason the proposal to add the phrase "with appropriate speed and efficiency" (that had been initially supported) was rejected since it would involve the court in reviewing whether a particular step at a particular time was or was not necessary.

Section 14 (*Failure or impossibility to Act*)

The Section (as amended by Act 3 of 2016) generally follows Article 14.

***

Article 15 *of the Model Law (Appointment of Substitute Arbitrator)*

This Article has a dual function:

First, it provides a mechanism for appointing substitute arbitrators.
Second, it also expresses two principles respecting termination of an arbitrator's mandate:

(i) that parties may agree to terminate the mandate of an arbitrator for any reason

(ii) the arbitrator may resign (also) for any reason.

The parties were left free to adopt any procedure for appointing a replacement arbitrator; it states that "a substitute arbitrator shall be appointed "according to the rules that were applicable to the appointment of the arbitrator being replaced".

Unlike the UNCITRAL Arbitration Rules, the Model Law does not contain any provision on whether the replacement arbitrator appointed under Article 15, should rehear witnesses and arguments at the new hearing. That was left to be considered as a matter of arbitral procedure.

Section 15 *of the* 1996 *Act*—(Termination of mandate and Substitution of Arbitrator)

Although Section 15 is differently worded, though the intent is the same as that stated in the Article viz:

(i) that the mandate of the arbitrator terminates when he withdraws from office for any reason

(ii) or a pursuant to agreement of parties.

Section 15(3) additionally provides that whenever the arbitrator is replaced, hearings previously held "may be repeated at the discretion of the arbitral tribunal." In addition, Section 15(4) states that a change of composition of the arbitral tribunal will not invalidate any order or ruling of the tribunal prior, to the replacement of an arbitrator.

***

Chapter—IV: Jurisdiction of Arbitral Tribunal—Sections 16 and 17

Chapter IV of the Model Law contains Articles 16 and 17.

While Article 16 provides for the "Competence of arbitral tribunal to rule on its own jurisdiction", Article 17 deals with the power of the arbitral tribunal to order interim measures.

The first sentence in paragraph (1) of Article 16 that "the arbitral tribunal may rule on its own jurisdiction including any objections with respect to the existence of the validity of the arbitration agreement" is modelled on Article 21(1) of the UNCITRAL Arbitration Rules.

Article 16 articulates the principle of *Kompetenz-kompetenz*, which means that an arbitral tribunal is competent to rule on its own competence. The power of arbitral tribunals to decide on questions going to jurisdiction has been widely accepted, as for instance in the UNCITRAL Arbitration Rules (Article 21(1)), and Rules for the International Chamber of Commerce (ICC) Court of Arbitration (Article 8(3) as well as in the Washington Convention (ICSID) (Article 41(1). This is an important concept in practice, because without it a party could stall the arbitration merely by *raising* a jurisdictional objection that could get resolved only in prolonged court proceedings.

Under Article 16, an arbitral tribunal's power is circumscribed. It is neither exclusive nor final. Its decision under the Model Law is subject to an immediate review by a court under Article 16(3). And only later, to a further court-review in the setting-aside procedure under Article 34. And ultimately—to a further review in an action for recognition and enforcement under Article 36.

Under Article 16, the arbitral tribunal has a choice whether to decide a jurisdictional question at a preliminary stage or only in the final award.

The principle of *Kompetenz-kompetenz*, (it may be noted) is mandatory. Parties cannot agree to limit the power of the arbitral tribunal to rule on its own jurisdiction.

Despite the fact that an amendment to add the phrase "unless otherwise agreed by the parties" at the beginning of the paragraph–(I) was not adopted, in the report of the Working Group, it was however noted (by the Working Group) that the state that adopted the Model Law "might provide" that parties could eliminate or limit the tribunal's power in this respect.[29]

Section 16_in Chapter IV (Jurisdiction of Arbitral Tribunals) of the 1996 Act follows Article 16 of the Model Law but with a difference. In the Model Law on a plea made by one of the parties questioning the jurisdiction of the arbitral tribunal and the arbitral tribunal ruling it has jurisdiction, any party may request the court (the court mentioned in Article 6 of the Model Law)[30] to decide the matter viz. whether the arbitral tribunal has jurisdiction and its decision is not subject to further appeal. But, in Section 16 of the Act, there is a departure. On a plea made by a party questioning the jurisdiction of the arbitral tribunal and the arbitral tribunal accepting the plea, an appeal under Section 37(2)(a) of the Act is expressly provided-for. However, if the arbitral tribunal rejects the plea and proceeds with the arbitration, the aggrieved party has no immediate remedy. The only recourse for the party is to make an application for setting aside the arbitral award after the award is passed by the Tribunal under Section 34 of the 1996 Act. In its recent decision in *Indian Farmers Fertilizer Co-Operative Limited* vs. *Bhadra Products* (AIR 2018 S.C. 627, at page 635), the Supreme Court of India has commented on the *Kompetenz-Kompetenz* principle:

> "The *Kompetenz principle* which is also followed by the English Arbitration Act, 1996, is that the word 'jurisdiction' mentioned in Section 16 has reference to three things:

(i) as to whether there is the existence of a valid arbitration agreement;

(ii) whether the arbitral tribunal is properly constituted; and

(iii) matters submitted to the arbitration should be in accordance with the arbitration agreement, 'jurisdiction' being a coat of many colours."

"In the case of *Uttrakhand Purv Sainik Kalyan Nigam Limited* vs. *Northern Coal Field Ltd.*, reported in 2019 (6) SCALE 696, a Bench of 2 judges of the Supreme Court of India has held that in view of Section 16 and the legislative policy to restrict judicial intervention at the pre-reference stage, an issue of limitation would require to be decided by the Arbitral Tribunal."

However, under Section 16 of the Act—as under Article 16 of the Model Law—there is no compulsion on an arbitral tribunal to decide a jurisdictional question at a preliminary stage. This is because in every case the arbitral tribunal has to assess whether the request to decide such a jurisdictional question at a preliminary stage is a dilatory tactic or a genuine one—and because it must keep in mind that time and money (in the arbitration) is not wasted.

***

Article 17 *of the Model Law* (*Power of Arbitral Tribunal to Order Interim Measures as revised by the UNCITRAL Amendment of 2006*)

Like Article 26 of the UNCITRAL Arbitration Rules, this too deals with *interim measures* but in a more detailed fashion due to the concern about maintaining the efficacy of the arbitral process and of the ultimate award. The UNCITRAL Commission when approving the 2006 amendments to the Model Law 1985 stated:

> "88. The Commission recalled that the provisions had been drafted in recognition not only that interim measures were increasingly being found in the practice of international commercial arbitration, but also that the effectiveness of arbitration as a method of settling commercial disputes depended on the possibility of enforcing such interim measures (se A/CN. 9/485 and Corr. 1, para 78). General agreement was expressed as to the need for a harmonized and widely acceptable model legislative regime governing interim measures granted by arbitral tribunals and their enforcement, as well as interim measures ordered by courts in support of arbitration.[31]

Section 17 (Interim Measures ordered by the arbitral tribunal) had been differently worded in the 1996 Act when enacted, but by Amending Act 3 of 2016,[32] it had been substituted following upon an important provision mentioned in the amended Model Law of 2006. The amended provision follows the amended Model Law of 2006, and from July 2019 it now provides as follows:

(1) "A party may, during the arbitral proceedings[33], apply to the arbitral tribunal:

(i) for the appointment of a guardian for a minor or person of unsound mind for the purposes of arbitral proceedings; or

(ii) for an interim measure of protection in respect of any of the following matters, namely:

(a) the preservation, interim custody or sale of any goods which are the subject-matter of the arbitration agreement;

(b) securing the amount in dispute in the arbitration;

(c) the detention, preservation or inspection of any property or thing which is the subject-matter of the dispute in arbitration, or as to which any question may arise therein and authorising for any of the aforesaid purposes any person to enter upon any land or building in the possession of any party, or authorising any samples to be taken, or any observation to be made, or experiment to be tried, which may be necessary or expedient for the purpose of obtaining full information or evidence;

(d) interim injunction or the appointment of a receiver;

(e) such other interim measure of protection as may appear to the arbitral tribunal to be just and convenient, and the arbitral tribunal shall have the same power for making orders, as the Court has for the purpose of, and in relation to, any proceedings before it."

(2) Subject to any orders passed in an appeal under section 37, any order issued by the arbitral tribunal under this section shall be deemed to be an order of the Court for all purpose and shall be enforceable under the Code of Civil Procedure, 1908 (5 of 1908), in the same manner as if it were an order of the Court.

It has been mentioned by the Supreme court of India—in *Alka Chandewar* vs *Shamshul Ishrar Khan* 2017 (16) SCC 119—that sub-section (2) had been added (in July 2019) so that the cumbersome procedure of the arbitral tribunal having to apply every time to the High Court for contempt of its orders would not be necessary. Hence, such orders are now deemed to be orders of the court for all purposes, to be enforced under the CPC, 1908, in the same manner as if they were the orders of the court.[34]

The Supreme Court of India has recently held that a tribunal like the Gujarat Public Works Contract Disputes Arbitration Tribunal constituted under the Gujarat Act of 1992, has jurisdiction to make interim orders in terms of Section 17 of the Arbitration and Conciliation Act, 1996: *State of Gujarat, Through Chief Secretary* vs. *Amber Builders* reported in 2020 (1) SCALE 618.

***

Chapter-V: Conduct of Arbitral Proceedings—Sections 18 to 27

Article 18 of the Model Law ("i.e. parties shall be treated with equality and each party shall be given a full opportunity of presenting his case") is the shortest of all the Articles in the Model Law—*but the most important.* It is rightly described (along with Article 19) as a key element, the "Magna Carta of Arbitration Procedure". It is the "due process clause" of all arbitrations.

Its object had been stated in the Secretariat Note on possible features of a Model Law (in May 1981) in which it had been observed:

> "73. The Model Law should empower the arbitral tribunal to conduct the arbitration proceedings in such manner as it considers appropriate, subject to the following restrictions. The arbitral tribunal must treat the parties with equality and give each party at any stage of the proceedings a full opportunity of presenting his case. . ."

The understanding of the Working Group was that Article 18 should apply to all stages of the arbitral proceedings.

Section 18 of the Act of 1996 is a replica of Article 18. It is extremely important because a party's inability to present its case is a separate ground for setting aside the arbitral award under Section 34 (2) (iii).

***

Article 19 *of the Model Law* (*Determination of Rules of Procedure*)

It establishes the autonomy of the parties and of the arbitrators in the procedural conduct of the arbitration. It expresses confidence in the ability of the parties and the arbitrators to conduct the arbitration in a fair and orderly manner so as to arrive at a just resolution of a dispute. The autonomy principle is critical to an effective system of commercial arbitration for international cases because in these cases there is need to be *free of local standards*.

Section 19 of the 1996 Act (Determination of Rules of Procedure) is the Indian counter-part of Article 19 of the Model Law—Sub-clause (1) of which makes clear that—because the parties are free to agree on the procedure to be followed by the tribunal, "the arbitral tribunal shall not be bound by the Code of Civil Procedure 1908 or the Indian Evidence Act 1872[35].

***

Article 20 *of the Model Law* (*Place of Arbitration*)

The parties are free to agree on the place of arbitration.

Section 20 of the 1996 Act is a mechanical reproduction of Article 20 of the Model Law. Section 20(1) ("the parties are free to agree on the place of arbitration") has to be read along with, and is controlled by, the general provision already enacted in Section 2(2) (Chapter-I: General Provisions)—"This part shall apply where the *place of arbitration is in India*". Since the entire Part-I is governed by the requirement that the place of arbitration be in India, the language used in Section 20 of the Act is tautologous.

The *venue* of an Arbitration proceeding—which can be anywhere—must never be confused with the "*place of arbitration*". This is how the decision of the Supreme Court of India in *Sanshin Chemicals Industry* vs. *Oriental Carbons and Chemicals Ltd.* reported in (2001) 3 SCC 341 = AIR 2001 S.C. 1219 is to be read and understood[36]. In that case Japan was the designated place of arbitration but the venue of arbitration had to be determined by some third party, and the only question for the court was whether the decision of the third party determining the venue was or was not an "award". Other important cases distinguishing between "seat" of arbitration and the "venue" of an arbitration, are: *Enercon (India) Ltd and Ors.* vs. *Enercon Gmbh and Anr* reported in AIR 2014 SC 3152 (in particular paragraph 90); and *Union of India* vs. *Hardy Exploration and Production India Ltd.*, reported in AIR 2018 SC 4871.

***

Article 21 *of the Model Law* (*Commencement of arbitral proceedings*)

This has its counterpart in Section 21 of the Act (Commencement of arbitral proceedings) and so also Article 22 (Language) whose corresponding provision in the Act is Section 22.

In *Sundaram Finance Ltd.* vs. *NEPC:* AIR 1999 SC 565 it had been stated:

> "The reading of Section 21 clearly shows that the arbitral proceedings commence on the date on which a request for a dispute to be referred to arbitration is received by the respondent. Section 21 is of relevance in connection with the previous of limitation under Section 43 and the savings provisions in Section 85(2)(a)."

Section 21 *of the 1996 Act* (*Commencement of arbitral proceedings*) — *when a request for that dispute to be referred is received by the respondent.*

Section 22 *of the 1996 Act* (*Language*): gives freedom to the parties upon the language or languages to be used in the arbitral proceedings. Failing such agreement, the arbitral tribunal is required to determine the language or languages to be used in the arbitral proceedings. The freedom of the tribunal in this regard is subject to Section 18 which provides that the parties shall be treated with equality and that each party shall be given a full opportunity to present his case. In the matter of determination of the language or languages, the tribunal may take into consideration the following factors, among others:

(a) the need for using more than one language

(b) the language capabilities of the parties and of the arbitrators,

(c) the costs of the arbitration if more than one language is to be used and the language employed by the parties in their business dealings with each other.

***

Article 23 of the Model Law (Statements of Claim and Defence)

On the legislative history of Article 23 (Statement of Claim and Defence) it has been stated by Holtzmann and Neuhaus at page 646 in their *A Guide to the UNCITRAL Model Law on International Commercial Arbitration*, 1989, that the legislative history of Article 23, particularly the discussion in the Commission, was dominated by two questions:

(i) the extent to which the rules set out in paragraph 1 relating to the contents of the statements of claim and defence were to be regarded as mandatory or non-mandatory, and, whether the parties could agree to the contrary; and

(ii) the extent to which the arbitral tribunal was to limit a party's right to amend its claim or defence during the course of the arbitral proceedings.

On both issues, the Commission adopted an effective compromise as the minimum (but essential) requirement. It was in this sense that Article 23 of the Model Law was stated to be non-mandatory.

Section 23 of the 1996 Act (Statement of Claim and Defence) corresponds to Article 23 of the Model Law. In Section 23, sub-section 2A has been added by Amending Act No. 3 of 2016 to provide, additionally, for a counter claim or set off.[37]

By the Arbitration and Conciliation (Amendment) Act No. 33 of 2019, sub-section (4) has been also added to Section 23, which now reads as follows:

> "(4) The Statement of Claim and Defence under this Section shall be completed within a period of six months from the date the arbitrator or all the arbitrators, as the case may be, received notice in writing of their appointment". (added in the interest of speeding-up the arbitration).

***

Article 24 *of the Model Law* (*Hearing and Written Proceedings*)

This gives expression to two basic rules:

(i) if a party requests a hearing the arbitral tribunal must provide a hearing;

(ii) if no party requests a hearing, it is for the arbitral tribunal to hold a hearing or not hold a hearing.

When a proposal was made in the Working Group (drafting the Model Law) that a party should have a right to request oral argument only "on the substance of the dispute, and not on procedural or jurisdictional questions," the Working Group expressed its opposition to this suggestion, and the proposal was not added.

Section 24 *of the* 1996 *Act* (Hearing and written proceedings) has adopted Article 24 of the Model Law, except that by the amending Act 3 of 2016, it has been additionally provided that "the arbitral tribunal shall, as far as possible, hold oral hearings for the presentation of evidence or for oral argument on a day-to-day basis and not grant any adjournments unless sufficient cause be made out, and may impose costs including exemplary costs on the parties seeking adjournment without any sufficient cause." (this again, in the interest of speeding-up the arbitration).

Article 25 of the Model Law (Default of a Party)

Under this Article, unless otherwise agreed by the parties, if without showing sufficient cause the claimant fails to communicate his statement of claim or the respondent fails to communicate his statement of defence—as required by the arbitral tribunal—express provision has been made for the arbitral tribunal to continue the proceedings without treating such failure in itself as an admission of the claimant's allegations.

Similarly, if any party fails to appear at a hearing or to produce documentary evidence the arbitral tribunal is empowered to continue the proceedings and make the award on the evidence before it. When the secretariat of UNCITRAL first addressed this topic, it stated that "an arbitral law must provide arbitration with its necessary teeth" (see page 698 of Holtzmann and Neuhaus *A Guide to the UNCITRAL Model Law on International Commercial Arbitration.*) The Commission did not address the question whether a tribunal could draw adverse inferences from a failure of a party to appear or produce an evidence or prove documentary evidence. But the comment of the UNCITRAL secretariat was that "the arbitral tribunal is not precluded from drawing adverse inferences from a party not

producing any evidence as requested." The UNCITRAL secretariat had also noted that the power under Clause (c) of Article 25 (where any party fails to appear at a hearing or to produce documentary evidence, the arbitral tribunal may continue the proceedings and make the award on the evidence before it) would include the power to disregard evidence that is tendered after the specified time limit.
Section 25 *of the* 1996 *Act* (Default of a Party) is a reproduction of Article 25 of the UNCITRAL Model Law. It has been held by the Supreme Court of India in *Shri Infrastructure Finance Limited* vs. *Tuff Drilling Pvt. Ltd.*: (2018) 11 SCC 470 that the scheme of Section 25 of the 1996 Act, indicates that on sufficient cause being shown, the statement of claim could be permitted to be filed even after the time fixed by Section 23(1)—for filing the same—had expired (at para 23).

***

Article 26 *of the Model Law* (*An Expert to be appointed by Arbitral Tribunal*)

This has been modelled on Article 27 of the UNCITRAL Arbitration Rules. Power of the arbitral tribunal to appoint experts of course may be altered by agreement of the parties, and where an arbitral tribunal appoints an expert each party is free to present its own expert as a witness.

Section 26 *of the* 1996 *Act* (Expert appointment by the arbitral tribunal) follows Article 26 of the Model Law.

***

Article 27 of the Model Law (Court assistance in taking evidence)

Article 27 only provides that the arbitral tribunal or a party with the approval of the arbitral tribunal may request from a competent court of the state, assistance in taking evidence and the court may execute the request within its competence and according to its rules on taking evidence.

Article 27 had been a troublesome provision for the Working Group as well as for the Commission, with some members of the Working Group raising the problem of recourse to courts being abused for purposes of delay, and also (in some countries) envisaging the impossibility of securing assistance from courts. There were three concerns expressed in the Working Group:

(i) integration with existing court procedures;

(ii) possibility of abuse;

(iii) Court assistance.

The resolution of these concerns helped to shape the final text of Article 27. The Hague Conference on Private International Law in 1970, had examined whether the Hague Convention on Taking of Evidence Abroad in Civil or Commercial Matters should also cover arbitral proceedings, but the Working Group reached no definite conclusion on this since it expressed doubts about its usefulness.

Section 27 *of the* 1996 *Act* (Court Assistance in taking evidence) is far more detailed than Article 27 of the Model Law (the section has been reproduced in the endnote)[38]. In *Delta Distillers Ltd.* vs. *United Spirits Limited and Anr: AIR 2014 SC 113* the Supreme Court of India held that Section 27 empowers the arbitral tribunal to seek assistance from a court for taking evidence. Whenever assistance is required, the tribunal ought to receive it, and it is for that purpose that this enabling provision (Section 27) is made in the Act.

***

Chapter VI: Arbitral Awards and Termination Proceedings—Sections 28 to 33

Article 28 *of the Model Law* (*Rules applicable to substance of dispute*)

This provides for rules that are *in* line with (the generally accepted modern theory and practice) of party autonomy: parties being free to choose any rules to govern the substance of the dispute even where the rules are territorially not connected with the contract or the dispute. (The secretariat of the Commission had noted that this approach was "at present widely, but not yet uniformly, adopted").

It was felt by the Working Group that there was little reason for limiting the parties' choice by what rules the substance of the disputes were to be governed. The Commission report had noted that there was wide support for the view that the Model Law would be incomplete without a provision on rules applicable to the substance of the dispute, particularly in view of the fact that the Model Law dealt with international commercial arbitration where a lack of rules on that issue would give rise to uncertainty.

In Article 28, it is provided that the arbitral tribunal shall decide the dispute in accordance with such rules of law as are chosen by the parties as applicable to the substance of the dispute, and failing any designation by the parties the arbitral tribunal shall apply the law determined by the conflict of law rules as considered applicable and the arbitral tribunal shall decide ex aequo et bono or as amiable compositeur only if parties have necessarily authorised it to do so, and generally in all cases the arbitral tribunal shall decide in accordance with the terms of the contract and take into account the usages of trade applicable to the transaction.

Section 28 *of the* 1996 *Act* (Rules applicable to the substance of the dispute) though it has the same heading, is differently worded from Article 28; the emphasis in the section enacted is on the opening words "where the place of arbitration is situated in India") Section 28 reads:

"Where the place of the arbitration is situated in India

(a) in an arbitration other than an international commercial arbitration (as defined in Section 2(f)), the arbitral tribunal shall decide the dispute submitted to arbitration in accordance with the substantive law for the time being in force in India.

(b) in international commercial arbitration

(i) the arbitral tribunal shall decide the dispute in accordance with the rules of law designated by the parties as applicable to the substance of the dispute;

(ii) any designation by the parties of the law or legal system of a given country shall be construed, unless otherwise expressed, as directly referring to the substantive law of that country and not to its conflict of laws rules;

(iii) failing any designation of the law under clause (a) by the parties, the arbitral tribunal shall apply the rules of law it considers to be appropriate given all the circumstances surrounding the dispute. It is clear from Section 28 that it is premised on place of arbitration being situated in India and not abroad—the definition of international commercial arbitration in the Act has no reference at all to arbitrations situated in places outside India.

(2) the arbitral tribunal shall decide *ex acquo et bono* or as *amiable compositeur* only if the parties have expressly authorised it to do so;

(3) While deciding and making an award, the arbitral tribunal shall, in all cases, take into account the terms of the contract and trade usages applicable to the transaction."

Sub-section (3) has been added by Amending Act No. 3 of 2016 (viz. while deciding and making an award the arbitral tribunal shall in all cases take into account the terms of the contract and trade usages applicable to the transaction). Before sub-section (3) had been added, in the case of *Associate Builders* vs. *DDA*: (2015) 3 SCC 51, the Supreme Court of India had observed that the construction of the terms of the contract was primarily for an arbitrator to decide, unless the arbitrator had construed the contract in such a way that it could be said to be something that no fair minded or reasonable person could do. In its later decision (8 May 2019)—after Clause (3) had been added to Section 28 by the Amending Act No. 3 of 2016—the Supreme Court of India reiterated (in *Ssangyong Engineering* vs. *NHAI*[39] that Section 28(3) (as added by the Amendment Act No. 3 of 2016) follows what had been already observed in its earlier judgment in *Associated Builders* vs. *DDA*: (2015) 3 SCC 5, that the construction of the terms of the contract was primarily for an arbitrator to decide.

***

Article 29 *of the Model Law* (Decision making by panel of arbitrators) was modelled on Article 31 of the UNCITRAL Arbitration Rules

It provides for a decision by majority if there is more than one arbitrator with questions of procedure being decided by the presiding arbitrator.[40]

Section 29 *of the* 1996 *Act* (Decision making by a panel of arbitrators) corresponds to Article 29 of the Model Law which also provides that if authorised by the parties or by all the members of the arbitral tribunal, questions of procedure may be decided by the presiding arbitrator.

***

Making of Arbitral Award and Termination of Proceedings) provides for three *new sections*—29A, 29B and 31A—not provided for in the Model Law which had been inserted by the Amending Act No. 3 of 2016 (and still further amended in July 2019) with a view to expedite proceedings and eliminate, as far as possible, the perennial problem of delay in arbitral proceedings:

New Sections:

(I) Section 29A (Time Limit for arbitral awards) that had been added by the Amendment Act No. 3 of 2016, consisted of nine sub-clauses and sub-section (1) had provided that the 'award shall be made within a period of 12 months from the date the arbitral tribunal entered upon the reference'. By the further amendment of July 2019— the Arbitration and Conciliation (Amendment) Act No.33 of 2019, sub-section (1) and (4) have been substituted and Section 29A *now* reads as follows:

> "29A (1) The award in matters other than international commercial arbitration shall be made by the arbitral tribunal within a period of twelve months from the date of completion of pleadings under sub-section (4) of section 23.

Provided that the award in the matter of international commercial arbitration may be made as expeditiously as possible and endeavour may be made to dispose off the matter within a period of twelve months from the date of completion of pleadings under sub-section (4) of section 23.

(2) If the award is made within a period of six months from the date the arbitral tribunal enters upon the reference, the arbitral tribunal shall be entitled to receive such amount of additional fees as the parties may agree.

(3) The parties may, by consent, extend the period specified in sub-section (1) for making award for a further period not exceeding six months

(4). If an award is made within the period specified in sub-section (1) or the extended period specified under sub-section (3), the mandate of the arbitrator(s) shall terminate unless the court has, either prior to or after the expiry of the period so specified extended the period:

Provided that while extending the period under this sub-section, if the court finds that the proceedings have been delayed for the reasons attributable to the arbitral tribunal then it may order reduction of fees of the arbitrator (not exceeding 5 per cent), for each month of such delay;

Provided further that where an application under sub-section (5) is pending the mandate of the arbitrator shall continue till the disposal of the said application;

Provided also that the arbitrator shall be given an opportunity of being heard before the fee is reduced.

(5) The extension of period referred to in sub-section (4) may be on the application of any of the parties and may be granted only for sufficient cause and on such terms and conditions as may be imposed by the court.

(6) While extending the period referred to in sub-section (4), it shall be open to the court to substitute one or all of the arbitrators and if one or all of the arbitrators are substituted, the arbitral proceedings shall continue from the stage already reached and on the basis of the evidence and material already on record, and the arbitrator(s) appointed under this section shall be deemed to have received the said evidence and material.

(7) In the event of arbitrator(s) being appointed under this section, the arbitral tribunal thus reconstituted shall be deemed to be in continuation of the previously appointed arbitral tribunal.

(8) It shall be open to the court to impose actual or

exemplary costs upon any of the parties under this section.

(9) An application filed under sub-section (5) shall be disposed of by the court as expeditiously as possible and endeavour shall be made to dispose of the matter within a period of sixty days from the date of service of notice on the opposite party."

(II) Section 29B (Fast Track Procedure)—parties to an arbitration agreement are permitted at any stage either before or at the time of appointment of the arbitral tribunal to agree in writing to have their dispute resolved by a Fast Track Procedure specified in Section 29B (3)—i.e. that disputes be decided on the basis of written pleadings, documents and submissions without an oral hearing with power to the arbitral tribunal to call for any further information or clarification; and an oral hearing may be held only if all the parties make a request and the tribunal considers it necessary to have an oral hearing for clarifying certain issues. Power is also conferred on the arbitral tribunal to dispense with any technical formality, the object being an expeditious disposal of the dispute. The award under this Fast Track Procedure is to be made within a period of six months from the date the arbitral tribunal enters upon the reference.

The f*ast track arbitration* is one thing about which we in India (and in the entire Asian region) need to be better informed, because an alternative system of ultra-expeditious arbitrations has been tried and found workable elsewhere. But fast track arbitrations are successful only when they are approached by both parties in the right spirit. The show piece (in that regard) is the now famous ICC award of Prof. Hans Schmidt, where the Chairman of an ICC appointed arbitral tribunal, who with his colleagues delivered an award in a multi-million dollar arbitration in less than a month from the date of the tribunal's appointment, leaving the long-term contract intact between the parties. This was greatly facilitated by the parties carefully following fundamental criteria for drafting the arbitration agreement. (It is said that intelligent litigants usually craft their rules with deference to the adage that one person's delay is another's due process!).

The agreement must be clear enough to produce mandatory consequences for the parties, drafted with enough care so as to avoid the intervention of national courts; complete enough to give the arbitrators the power necessary to resolve the dispute; and coherent enough to put in place a procedure capable of rapidly and efficiently producing an enforceable award. The profound wisdom of these principles is only heightened by the pressures and demands of fast-track-arbitration. For more information on fast-track arbitration, attention is invited to an article by Benjamin Davis in the *Journal of International Arbitration*, December 1993, Vol. X, No. 4, page 69. Benajamin Davis was at that time a senior officer in the secretariat of the ICC, Paris and was monitoring this fast track arbitration on behalf of the ICC court. Davis had written:

> ". . . the worst delaying tactic that a party can use in a normal arbitration is the tactic of "overburdening the file". The arbitral tribunal has to wade through much chaff to get to the wheat—the heart of the parties' positions concerning the dispute. In a fast track arbitration (on the other hand) the time-pressure puts a premium on preparation, documentation being reduced only to the relevant and essential. Besides, in the fast-track setting, due to the importance of the dispute for both parties and the constraints of time, the pressure appears to push the parties in the opposite direction from overburdening the file."

(III) Section 31A (Regime for Costs) had also been included by amending Act No. 3 of 2016. The arbitral tribunal is empowered, notwithstanding anything contained in the Code of Civil Procedure 1908, at its discretion to determine whether costs are payable by one party to the other, the amount of such costs, and when they are to be paid. But it is has been clarified that the general rule is that the unsuccessful party shall be ordered to be paid the costs of the successful party. And if there is any departure from this rule, it is also provided that the arbitral tribunal may make a different order for reasons to be recorded in writing[41].

***

Article 30 *of the Model Law*

This Article provides for the procedure to be followed in the event that parties settle the dispute during the arbitral proceedings. The draftsmen of Article 30 fairly intended that both parties must agree to have a settlement converted into an award on agreed terms. But whether an arbitral tribunal had a discretion to refuse to record a settlement turned out to be a vexed question, when Article 30 was first drafted. At the Working Group meeting it appeared that although arbitrators would normally accede to a request by parties to enter the settlement in an award, they should not be compelled to do so in all circumstances (so stated in the First Working Group Report (paragraph 95, page 827 of Holtzman and Neuhaus: *A Guide to The UNCITRAL Model Law on International Commercial Arbitration—Legislative History and Commentary*, Kluwer Law and Taxation Publishers, Netherlands, 1995). The commission in its report has pointed out that the tribunal would object to a settlement only "in exceptional cases", such as binding laws of public policy including fundamental notions of fairness and justice (Commission Report A/40/70 paragraph 249).

Section 30 of the 1996 Act (Settlement) corresponds to Article 30 of the Model Law except that it also specifically provides that it is not incompatible with an arbitration agreement for an arbitral tribunal to encourage settlement of the dispute—a profound assertion of legislative policy. But more needs to be done in furtherance of legislative intent—by all arbitrators and all arbitral tribunals. Experience shows that an arbitral tribunal will record a settlement in the form of an arbitral award on agreed terms if during arbitral proceedings the parties themselves settle the dispute. But, in India (and elsewhere) arbitrators are reluctant to intercede and initiate or even attempt to bring about an overall settlement of the dispute. Attitudes need to change.

***

Article 31 *of the Model Law* (*Form and contents of the Award*)

It requires that the award shall state reasons upon which it is based unless the parties have agreed that no reasons are to be stated. And apart from stating its date and place of arbitration and a signed copy being delivered to each party, the right to issue a *dissenting opinion had been* a point in dispute in the Working Group and the commission. In the Working Group, the Norwegian delegate had urged and contended that a dissenting arbitrator was entitled to state his reasons for his dissent. Another delegate (from Sudan) contended that the award should not include any dissenting opinion/judgment. At the suggestion of the secretariat, the Commission was requested to take a decision as to whether a dissenting opinion would be permitted. But it did not address the question because according to Article 19 (Determination of Rules of Procedure) parties were free to agree on the procedure to be followed by the tribunal in conducting the proceedings.[42]

There is no tradition of dissenting opinions in the civil law system[43]; and dissenting opinions in international arbitration are traced to the common law tradition[44]—the only justification in the common law is that dissenting opinions may contribute to the development of the law[45]; but it is the decision of the majority that constitutes the award.

Section 31 of the 1996 Act (Form and Contents of the Arbitral Award) corresponds to Article 31 except that by the Amending Act No. 3 of 2016 Sub-clause 7(b) and Sub-clause (8) have been added— something not provided for in the Model Law—viz. that the sum directed to be paid by an arbitral award shall, unless the award otherwise directs, carry interest at the rate of 2 per cent higher than the current rate of interest prevalent on the date of the award, from the date of the award to the date of payment, and that the cost of an arbitration "shall be fixed" by the arbitral tribunal in accordance with Section 31(A) (which had been added by the Amending Act No. 3 of 2016 to provide for a regime for costs). In *Tamil Nadu Electricity Board* vs. *M/S. Bridge Tunnel Constructions:* 1997 (4) SCC 121 it has been stated by the Supreme Court of India that the award must state reasons in support of the determination of liability or non-liability. The following decisions of the Supreme Court of India relate to the award of interest *pendente lite: State of Haryana and Ors.* vs. *S.L. Arora and Company:* 2010 (3) SCC 690; *Union of India (UOI)* vs. *Ambica Construction:* AIR 2016 S.C. 1441; and *Chittaranjan Maity* vs. *Union of India*: AIR 2017 S.C. 4588.

[Section 31A Regime for Costs added by Amending Act No. 3 of 2016 has been dealt with earlier].

***

Articles 32 *and* 33 *of the Model Law:* (*Termination of Proceedings and Correction and Interpretation of Awards; additional award*)

Sections 32 *and* 33 *of the* 1996 *Act* (Termination of Proceedings and Correction and Interpretation of Award) correspond to Article 32 and 33 of the Model Law.

Where there is an advance agreement of parties setting out a deadline for an award, that deadline must be taken into account in issuing an order under Section 32(2)(b)[46] (Termination of Proceedings) because under Article 14(1) of the Model Law (corresponding to Section 14(1)(a) of the 1996 Act) the mandate of an arbitrator terminates when the arbitrator "fails to act without undue delay".

***

Chapter VII: Recourse Against Arbitral Awards—Section 34

Article 34 *of the Model Law* ("Application for setting aside as exclusive recourse against Arbitral Award") closely corresponds to (and is intended to correspond to) Article V of the New York Convention, 1958, since in the drafting of the Model Law, there were special instructions given that the Model Law, 1985 should closely follow the New York Convention, 1958.

The most difficult question was, of course, what grounds would justify setting aside an arbitral award. The primary issue here was whether the grounds for setting aside an award should be limited to those grounds on which recognition and enforcement of an award may be refused under the 1958 New York Convention on the Recognition and Enforcement of Foreign Arbitral Awards. The secretariat urged from the very beginning that the New York Convention grounds be incorporated into the Model Law's setting aside provision. As was said: "They are internationally accepted bases for attacking an award" and adopting them would help prevent . . . an international award [from] fall[ing] victim to local particularities of law."

The Working Group initially agreed. In view of the importance of the question, however, the Working Group and the Commission repeatedly revisited it and discussed it again at length. Numerous other possible grounds were considered. Each time, however, the conclusion to adopt the New York Convention grounds, with some relatively minor modifications, was reaffirmed.[47]

The grounds for setting aside, enumerated in Article 34(2), are essentially the same as those in the New York Convention. In several instances, however, the Working Group or the Commission modified the language used in the New York Convention but most of them were merely drafting changes.

In *M/s. Dyna Technologies Pvt. Ltd.*, vs. *M/s. Crompton Greaves Ltd.*, reported in 2020 (1) SCALE 121, a Bench of 3 judges of the Supreme Court has held that "inadequate reasoning" and basing its award on the approval of one of the parties, is not appropriate where complex issues are involved; the court has held that where an award is unintelligible it cannot be sustained.

But (by way of contrast) where an award was intelligible and the reasoning was adequate and the high court had refused to set it aside, a Bench of 3 judges of the Supreme Court had declined to interfere with the decision of the high court: *Vijay Trading and Transport Co.,* vs. *Central Warehousing Corporation*—reported in 2019 (16) SCALE 228.

Section 34 *of the* 1996 *Act* (Application for setting aside arbitral award) generally follows Article 34 of the Model Law, except for the addition of Explanation-I and Explanation II to Section 34(2)(b), as well as the addition of sub-section 2(A) (to Section 34) added by Amending Act No. 3 of 2016,[48]) for reasons stated in Clause 18 of the Bill (introducing the amending provisions):

> "Clause 18 of the Bill seeks to amend Section 34 of the principal Act to provide for explanation to the term 'public policy of India' in sub-clause (ii) of Clause (b) of sub-section (2) to the effect that an arbitral award shall be treated as an award in conflict with the public policy of India *only* where making of award was induced or affected by fraud or corruption or was in violation of Section 75 (Confidentiality) or Section 81 (Evidence in other proceedings) or is in contravention with the fundamental policy of Indian law; or it is in conflict with the most basic notions of morality or justice. Explanation 2 is inserted to explain that the test as to whether there is a contravention with the fundamental policy of Indian law shall not entail a review on the merits of the dispute. A new sub-section (2A) is inserted to provide an additional ground of patent illegality to challenge the arbitral award arising

out of arbitrations other than international commercial arbitrations."

Prior to July 2019 Section 34(2)(a), had followed the wording of the Model Law and stipulated that "an arbitral award may be set aside by the court only if:

"(a) The party making the application "*furnishes proof that*"..."

However, in July 2019, by the further amendment of the 1996 Act (Amending Act No. 33 of 2019) for the words "*furnishes proof that*" the words "*establishes on the basis of the record of the arbitral tribunal that*" were substituted. This substitution had its origin (and justification) in two decisions of the Supreme Court of India:

(i) in the case of *Fiza Developers and Inter-Trade Private Limited* vs. *AMCI (India) Private Limited and Another* (reported in 2009 (17) SCC 796), the court had deprecated the practice of framing issues under Section 34 of the 1996 Act, which appeared to be necessitated by the words "furnishes proof"; and

(ii) the case of *Emkay Global Financial Services Limited* vs. *Girdhar Sondhi reported in 2018 (9) SCC 49* it was stated that the nature of proceedings under Section 34 were summary.

The decision also stressed the need for expeditious disposal. In the latter decision, reported in 2018 (9) SCC

49), the recommendation of the high level committee (Justice Sri Krishna Committee)[49] (that the words "*establishes on the basis of the record of the arbitral tribunal that*" should be substituted in place of the words "*furnishes proof that*") received judicial benediction.

After the amendment of July 2019, by Amending Act No. 33 of 2019, Section 34(1) to Section 34(6) will now read as follows:

"34. Application for setting aside an arbitral award:

(1) Recourse to a court against an arbitral award may be made only by an application for setting aside such award in accordance with sub-section (2) and sub-section (3).

(2) An arbitral award may be set aside by the court only if:

(a) the party making the application establishes on the basis of the arbitral tribunal record that:

(i) a party was under some incapacity, or

(ii) the arbitration agreement is not valid under the law to which the parties have subjected it or, failing any indication thereon, under the law for the time being in force; or

(iii) the party making the application was not given proper notice of the appointment of an arbitrator or of the arbitral proceedings or was otherwise unable to present his case; or

(iv) the arbitral award deals with a dispute not contemplated by or not falling within the terms of the submission to arbitration, or it contains decisions on matters beyond the scope of the submission to arbitration. Provided that, if the decisions on matters submitted to arbitration can be separated from those not so submitted, only that part of the arbitral award which contains decisions on matters not submitted to arbitration may be set aside; or

(v) the composition of the arbitral tribunal or the arbitral procedure was not in accordance with the agreement of the parties, unless such agreement was in conflict with a provision of this Part from which the parties cannot derogate, or, failing such agreement, was not in accordance with this Part; or

(b) the court finds that:

(i) the subject-matter of the dispute is not capable of settlement by arbitration under the law for the time being in force, or

(ii) the arbitral award is in conflict with the public policy of India.

Explanation

1—For the avoidance of any doubt, it is clarified that an award is in conflict with the public policy of India, only if:

(i) the making of the award was induced or affected by fraud or corruption or was in violation of section 75 or section 81; or

(ii) it is in contravention with the fundamental policy of Indian law; or

(iii) it is in conflict with the most basic notions of morality or justice.

2—For the avoidance of doubt, the test as to whether there is a contravention with the fundamental policy of Indian law shall not entail a review on the merits of the dispute.

(2A) An arbitral award arising out of arbitrations other than international commercial arbitrations, may also be set aside by the court, if the court finds that the award is vitiated by patent illegality appearing on the face of the award. Provided that an award shall not be set aside merely on the ground of an erroneous application of the law or by re-appreciation of evidence.

3—An application for setting aside may not be made after three months have elapsed from the date on which the party making that application had received the arbitral award, or, if a request had been made under section 33, from the date on which that request had been disposed of by the arbitral tribunal. Provided that if the court is satisfied that the applicant was prevented by sufficient cause from making the application within the said period of three months, it may entertain the application within a further period of thirty days, but not thereafter.

4—On receipt of an application under sub-section (1), the court may, where it is appropriate and it is so requested by a party, adjourn the proceedings for a period of time determined by it in order to give the

> arbitral tribunal an opportunity to resume the arbitral proceedings, or to take such other action as in the opinion of arbitral tribunal will eliminate the grounds for setting aside the arbitral award.
> 5—An application under this section shall be filed by a party only after issuing a prior notice to the other party and such application shall be accompanied by an affidavit by the applicant endorsing compliance with the said requirement.
> 6—An application under this section shall be disposed of expeditiously, and in any event, within a period of one year from the date on which the notice referred to in sub-section (5) is served upon the other party."[50]

The grounds for setting aside, under Article 34 of the Model Law, though similar to Article V of the New York Convention, are not necessarily exhaustive and the state that adopts, or adapts, the UNCITRAL Model Law is free to prescribe additional grounds for setting aside a domestic award (as contrasted with "foreign awards"—in Chapter-I of Part-II (New York Convention Awards). Although courts and Parliament in India have followed the grounds set out in Article 34 of the Model law, in a particular case *Voltas Ltd.*, vs. *Rolta India Ltd.*, reported in 2014 (4) SCC 516 at page 533, paragraphs 32 and 33, the Supreme Court of India (without reference to any particular ground set out in Section 34) nullified and set aside an interim award for (what it characterised) as an "*incorrect and inappropriate appreciation of the proposition of law set out in a prior Supreme Court decision*":[51]

Upto July 2019, in application for setting aside domestic awards (including awards in "international commercial arbitration" as defined) the following decisions have been handed down by courts in India under Section 34 of the 1996 Act, on the grounds mentioned in Section 34(2):

(a) In the endnote[52] are listed cases in which domestic awards, under the 1996 Act, that *have been set aside* by the Supreme Court of India; they are relatively few.

(b) In the next endnote[53] are cases in which domestic awards, under the 1996 Act, had been initially set aside by high courts, but their decisions have been reversed by the Supreme Court of India. As a consequence, the domestic awards, though challenged, were ultimately not set aside.

(c) In the next endnote[54] are cases where recourse was taken to courts against domestic awards (for them to be set-aside)—but each such recourse has been unsuccessful. The domestic awards)—(in the cases listed in the endnote)—that had been challenged in courts, were not set aside.

***

Chapter VIII: Enforcement of Awards—Articles 35 and 36

Article 35 of the Model Law—"Recognition and Enforcement".

In Article 35 of the Model Law "An arbitral award, irrespective of the country in which it was made, shall be recognised as binding and, upon application in writing to the competent court, shall be enforced subject to the provisions of this article and of Article 36."[55]

The most important reason in favour of retaining provisions on recognition and enforcement in the Model Law, despite the matter having been dealt with by the New York Convention 1958, was that by having a single set of provisions for both foreign and domestic awards, the Model Law would have served to de-emphasise the importance of the place of arbitration in international commercial arbitration. This would have furthered the cause of harmonising worldwide arbitration law. In addition, it was said that without Article 35, the Model Law would be incomplete; without provisions on recognition and enforcement that would cover awards not governed by the New York Convention or some other multilateral or bilateral treaty— perhaps the true and only rationale for Article 35 as drafted. Few countries have adopted Article 35.

A "foreign award", to which the provisions of Part-II of the 1996 Act, do not apply—that is, a non-convention award—can now be enforced not under the 1996 Act (as Article 35 of the Model Law would have permitted if it had been adopted by India). Such a non-convention foreign award can now be enforced dehors the 1996 Act—that is, by filing a suit on the foreign award either under the common law or (more effectively) under the provision enacted in Section 9 of the Code of Civil Procedure, because Section 9 recognises a statutory right to file any suit of a civil nature in an appropriate court in India having jurisdiction.

Section 35 of the Act (*Finality of Arbitral Awards*) is a provision entirely different from Article 35 of the Model Law.

It states that subject to this Part (i.e. Part-I), an arbitral award shall be final and binding on the parties and persons claiming under them. In *Cheran Properties* vs. *Kasturi & Sons*: (2018) 16 SCC 413—a case under Section 35 of the 1996 Act—it was said that the provision of Section 35 would include cases of devolution and assignment of interest. The provision has been included (the court said) to widen the net to cover those who are not parties but whom the award binds. Thus, the provision making an arbitral award final and binding on the parties 'and persons claiming under them, "is a legislative recognition of the doctrine that an arbitral award binds not only parties but every person whose capacity or position is derived from and is the same as the party to the proceedings."

***

Article 36 of the Model law ("Grounds for Refusing" Recognition or Enforcement").

Article 36 is closely modelled on the New York Convention and goes further. It applies not only to arbitral awards issued outside the state in which enforcement or recognition is sought but also to non-domestic awards i.e. awards issued in international commercial arbitrations taking place in the enforcing or recognising state (as in the USA). This choice of an identical treatment, of so called non-domestic and foreign awards, was central to the effort to unify arbitration law. It was also in tune with UNCITRAL's initial decision to prepare the Model Law (adopted in June 1979) when the secretary-general was instructed that the draft Model Law should take into account the provisions of the 1958 New York Convention.

Since *Section* 36 of the Act is located in Part-I and Section 2(2) provides that Part-I shall apply where the place of arbitration is in India, the provision made in Section 36 ("Enforcement")—after its substitution for Section 36 as enacted (by Amending Act 3 of 2016)—is entirely different from Article 36 of the Model Law. It reads:

> "36(1) Where the time for making an application to set aside the arbitral award under section 34 has expired, then subject to the provisions of sub-section (2) such award shall be enforced in accordance with the provisions of the Code of Civil Procedure, 1908 (5 of 1908), in the same manner as if it were a decree of the court."

Section 36(2)—added by Amending Act No. 3 of 2016—provides that where an application to set aside the arbitral award has been filed in court under Section 34, the filing of such an application shall not by itself render that award unenforceable, unless the court grants an order of stay of the operation of the said arbitral award for reasons to be recorded in writing.

It has been noted by the Supreme Court of India in *BCCI* vs. *Kochi Cricket Pvt. Ltd.*: 2018 (6) SCC 287, that the provisions of Section 36 (as substituted by the Amending Act No. 3 of 2016), do not apply to proceedings pending at the time when the Amending Act No. 3 of 2016 was brought into force. These would remain to be governed by Section 36 (as had been originally enacted), which simply read as follows:

> "36. *Enforcement* where the time for making an application to set aside the arbitral award under Section 34 has expired or, such application having been made it has been refused, the award shall be enforced under the Code of Civil Procedure, 1908, in the same manner as if it were a decree of the court."

***

Chapter IX: Appeals—Section 37

Section 37 (*Appealable orders*)[56] finds its place in the 1996 Act as a consequential provision—it is peculiar to Indian law—and does not occur in the Model Law.

Under Section 37 of the 1996 Act, appeals lie from the following orders (and from no others) to the court authorised by law to hear appeals from original decrees of the court passing the order viz.

(a) refusing to refer parties to arbitration under Section 8;

(b) granting or refusing to grant any measure under Section 9; and

(c) setting aside or refusing to set aside an arbitral award under Section 34.

Appeals also lie to a court from an order of an arbitral tribunal accepting the plea referred is in Sections 16(2) and 16(3), as well as granting or refusing an interim measure under Section 17. No second appeal lies from an order passed in appeal, but this provision does not take away any right of appeal to the Supreme Court of India: as for instance under Article 136 of the Constitution of India.

It has been held: in *Deep Industries Ltd.,* vs. *Oil and Natural Gas Corporation Ltd.*, by a Bench of 3 judges of the Supreme Court of India reported in (2019) 17 SCALE page 85, that though petitions can be filed in high courts under Article 227 of the Constitution against judgments of lower courts allowing and dismissing first appeals under Section 37, yet high courts should be extremely circumspect in interfering with such decision because "the object of the 1996 Act, is that of minimising judicial intervention".

***

Chapter-X: Miscellaneous—Sections 38 to 43

Sections 38 to 43, in Chapter X are also consequential and find a place only in the 1996 Act (not in the Model Law). *Section* 38 deals with deposits;

Section 39 provides for lien on arbitral awards and deposit as to costs;

Section 40 provides that an arbitration agreement is not to be discharged by the death of the party thereto but be enforceable by or against the legal representative;

Section 41 makes provisions in case of insolvency;

Section 42 deals with the subject of "jurisdiction" of courts. Where any application is made to a court under Part-I, it is that court alone that has the jurisdiction in respect of all subsequent proceedings.

Reported decisions of the Supreme Court of India under or in respect of Section 42 (Jurisdiction) and Section 43 (Limitations) are noted below:

(1) Reported Decisions of the Supreme Court of India which make reference to Section 42 of the 1996 Act: (Jurisdiction) are the following:

Pandey and Co. Builders Pvt. Ltd. vs. *State of Bihar* 2007 (1) SCC 467 on appeal from 2006 (1) Arb. LR 429 (Patna); *Rodemadan India Ltd.* vs. *International Trade Expo Centre Ltd.* 2006 (11) SCC 651; *Rite Approach Group Ltd.* vs. *Rosoboron Export* 2006 (1) SCC 206 followed in *Standard Corrosion Controls (Pvt.) Ltd.* vs. *Sarku Engineering Services SDH BHD* 2009 (1) SCC 303; *Jindal Vijaynagar Steel (J.S.W. Steel Ltd.)* vs. *Jindal Praxair Oxygen Co. Ltd.* 2006 (11) SCC 521; *Nimet Resources* vs. *Essar*

Steels Ltd. 2007 (Supp.) Arb. LR 7 (S.C.); *NPCC Ltd.* vs. *Sadhu Singh* 2008 (7) SCC 778; *State of Mahrashtra* vs. *Atlanta Ltd.* 2014 (11) SCC 619; *State of West Bengal* vs. *Associated Contractors* AIR 2015 S.C. 260; *Bhandari Udyog Ltd.* vs. *Industrial Facilitation Council* 2015 (14) SCC 515; *Shree Baidyanath Ayurved Bhawan (Pvt.) Ltd.* vs. Praveen Bhatia 2009 (8) SCC 779; *Yograj Infrastructure Ltd.* vs. *Ssang Yong Engineering and Construction Co. Ltd.* 2011 (9) SCC 735; *Emkay Global Financial Services Ltd.* vs. *Girdhar Sondhi* 2018 (9) SCC 49 following Indus *Mobile Distribution (P) Ltd.* vs. *Datawind Innovations* (*P*) *Ltd.* 2017 (7) SCC 678.

(2) Reported decisions of the Supreme Court of India which make reference to Section 43 of the 1996 Act (Limitations) are set out below:

State of Goa vs. *Western Builders* 2006 (6) SCC 239; *J.C. Budhraja* vs. *Orissa Mining Corporation Ltd.* 2008 (2) SCC 444; *Assam Urban Water Supply and Sewerage Board* vs. *Subash Projects and Marketing Ltd.* 2012 (2) SCC 624; *Voltas Ltd.* vs. *Rolta India Ltd.* 2014 (4) SCC 516; *Indian Farmers Fertilizer Co-operative Ltd.* vs. *Bhadra Products* 2018 (2) SCC 534.

Sections 42A *and* 42B have been newly added by the further Amendment passed by both Houses of Parliament in July 2019 (Arbitration and Conciliation (Amendment) Act No. 33 of 2019) and they read as follows:

> 42A. Confidentiality of Information: Notwithstanding anything contained in any other law for the time being in force, the arbitrator, the arbitral institution and the parties to the arbitration agreement shall maintain confidentiality of all arbitral proceedings except an award where its disclosure is necessary for the purpose of implementation and enforcement of award.
>
> 42B. Protection of action taken in good faith: No suit or other legal proceedings shall lie against the arbitrator for anything which is in good faith done, or intended to be done, under this Act or the rules or regulations made thereunder.[57]

As regards insertion of Section 42A, this is in line with what the English courts have decided: that arbitration being 'essentially private' there is an implied obligation of confidentiality in arbitration agreements as a matter of law: so held in *Ali Shipping Corporation* vs. *Shipyard Togire*, reported in 1999 (1) Weekly Law Reports 314 (a decision of the UK Court of Appeals). The decision is also reported in 1998 (1) Lloyds Law Reports 643 CA.

The High Court of Australia however has rejected the English view; in Sweden, Norway and in the USA as well, the idea of a general implied duty of confidentiality in arbitration proceedings is not accepted. In an article that appeared in *Arbitration International* Vol. 15, No. 3, pages 211 to 225, Dr Gerald Herrmann ('father of the UNCITRAL Model Law 1985') had written:

> "Confidentiality is no longer presumed to be an implied term of an arbitration agreement—if you want it, you must now provide for it."

The Amendment of July 2019, (with the addition of Section 42A) now provides for it.

***

Case-Law: CLOUT (Case Law on UNCITRAL texts):

Part-I of India's 1996 Act (Arbitration) has been framed "taking into account" the UNCITRAL Model Law of 1985. Its contents are based on the International Commercial Arbitration Act of 1996 of British Columbia (Canada) which closely follows the UNCITRAL Model Law of 1985[58]. Decisions of courts in British Columbia (and ultimately of the Supreme Court of Canada) are relevant in India (where applicable).

—Peter Binder in the 4th edition of his book on the UNCITRAL Model Law has given the most recent decisions reported in CLOUT from (2015 to 2019). They are:[59]

(1) On Article 8: (Arbitration Agreement and Substantive Claim before Court):

- Case 1661 — Singapore/Court of Appeal: *Tomolugen Holdings Ltd. and Another vs. Silica Investors Ltd. and Other* appeals (26 October 2015) (A/CN.9/SER./C/ABSTRACTS/179).

(2) On Article 9: (Arbitration Agreement and Interim Measures by Court):

- *Case 1725*—United States of America/U.S. Court of Appeals, Eleventh Circuit: *SCL Basilisk AG* vs. *Agribusiness United Savannah Logistics*

LLC (14 November 2017) (A/CN. 9/SER. C/ABSTRACTS/187)

(3) On Article 18: (Equal Treatment of Parties):

- *Case 1660*—Singapore/High Court: *AMZ* vs. *AXX* (30 October 2015) (A/CN. 9/SER. C/ABSTRACTS/179)

(4) On Article 34: (Application for Setting Aside as Exclusive Recourse against Arbitral Award):

- *Case 1717*—Greece/Hellenic Supreme Court of Civil and Penal Justice: *Case No. 366/2016* (16 May 2016) (A/CN. 9/SER. C/ABSTRACTS/186).

- *Case 1718*—Paraguay/First Chamber of the Civil and Commercial Appeals Court of Asuncion: *Carnicas Villacuenca S.A.* vs. *Arbitral Process ntitled Yvu Poty S.A.* vs. *Pabensa S.A. and Carnicas Villacuenca S.A.* (29 December 2016) (A/CN. 9/SER. C/ABSTRACTS/186).

- *Case 1749*—India/Supreme Court: *Indian Farmers Fertilizer Cooperative Limited* vs. *Bhadra Products* (23 January 2018) (A/CN. 9/SER. C/ABSTRACTS/190).

- *Case 1755*—Australia/Supreme Court of Queensland (Court of Appeal): *Mango Boulevard*

Pty Ltd. vs. *Mio Art Pty Ltd. & Anor* (20 March 2018) (A/CN. 9/SER. C/ABSTRACTS/191).

- *Case 1535*—Singapore/High Court: *AQZ* vs. *ARA* (13 February 2015) (A/CN. 9/SER. C/ABSTRACTS/164).

- *Case 1649*—Canada/Superior Court of Justice of Ontario: *Consolidated* vs. *Ambatovy* (28 November 2016) (A/CN. 9/SER. C/ABSTRACTS/178).

- *Case 1651*—Canada/Court of Appeal of Ontario: *Popack* vs. *Lipszyc* (18 February 2016) (A/CN. 9/SER. C/ABSTRACTS/178).

- *Case 1659*—Singapore/High Court: *AYH* vs. *AYI and another* (23 November 2015) (A/CN. 9/ SER. C/ABSTRACTS/179).

- *Case 1652*—Canada's Superior Court of Justice in Ontario: *Jacob Securities Inc.* vs. *Typhoon Capital BV* (26 January 2016) (A/CN. 9/SER. C/ABSTRACTS/178).

(5) On Article 35: (Recognition and Enforcement)

- *Case 1650* – Superior Court of Justice of Ontario Canada: *Entes* vs. *Kyrgyz Republic* (16 November 2016) (A/CN. 9/SER. C/ABSTRACTS/178).

- *Case 1653* — Superior Court of Justice of Ontario in Canada: *Depo Traffic* vs. *Vikeda International* (18 February 2015) (A/CN. 9/SER. C/ABSTRACTS/178).

(6) On Article 36: (Grounds for Refusing Recognition and Enforcement)

- *Case 1653* — Superior Court of Justice of Ontario: *Depo Traffic* vs. *Vikeda International* (18 February 2015) (A/CN. 9/SER. C/ABSTRACTS/178).

- *Case 1650* — Superior Court of Justice of Ontario in Canada: *Entes* vs. *Kyrgyz Republic* (16 November 2016) (A/CN. 9/SER. C/ABSTRACTS/178).

End Notes:

1. Part-1A setting up of Arbitration Council of India and defining its duties and functions was included in the Arbitration and Conciliation (Amendment) Bill No: XXI of 2019, passed by both Houses of Parliament in July 2019, which became law upon assent to it given by the President. Part 1A, of course, is relatable to Part-I of the Act.
2. Corresponding to Articles 1 to 36 of the Model Law in Chapters I to VIII as below:

   Chapter I. General Provisions

   Article 1. Scope of application; Article 2. Definitions and rules of interpretation; Article 3. Receipt of written communications; Article 4. Waiver of right to object; Article 5. Extent of court intervention; Article 6. Court or other authority for certain functions of arbitration assistance and supervision.

Chapter II. Arbitration Agreement

Article 7. Definition and form of arbitration agreement; Article 8. Arbitration agreement and substantive claim before court; Article 9. Arbitration agreement and interim measures by court;

Chapter III. Composition of Arbitral Tribunal

Article 10. Number of arbitrators; Article 11. Appointment of arbitrators; Article 12. Grounds for challenge; Article 13. Challenge procedure; Article 14. Failure or impossibility to act; Article 15. Appointment of substitute arbitrator.

Chapter IV. Jurisdiction of Arbitral Tribunal

Article 16. Competence of arbitral tribunal to rule on its jurisdiction; Article 17. Power of arbitral tribunal to order interim measures.

Chapter V. Conduct of Arbitral Proceedings

Article 18. Equal treatment of parties; Article 19. Determination of rules of procedure; Article 20. Place of arbitration; Article 21. Commencement of arbitral proceedings; Article 22. Language; Article 23. Statements of claim and defence; Article 24. Hearings and written proceedings; Article 25. Default of a party; Article 26. Expert appointed by arbitral tribunal; Article 27. Court assistance in taking evidence.

Chapter VI. Making of Award and Termination of Proceedings

Article 28. Rules applicable to substance of dispute; Article 29. Decision making by panel of arbitrators; Article 30. Settlement; Article 31. Form and contents of award; Article 32. Termination of proceedings; Article 33.

Correction and interpretation of award additional award.
Chapter VII. Recourse Against Award
Article 34. Application for setting aside as exclusive recourse against arbitral award.
Chapter VIII. Recognition and Enforcement of Awards
Article 35. Recognition and enforcement;
Article 36. Grounds for refusing recognition or enforcement.

3. The UNCITRAL Model Law 1985 consists of Chapters-I to VIII viz.
   Chapter-I: General Provisions (Articles 1 to 6)
   Chapter-II: Arbitration Agreement (Articles 7 to 9)
   Chapter-III: Composition of Arbitral Tribunal (Articles 10 to 15)
   Chapter-IV: Jurisdiction of Arbitral Tribunal (Articles 16 and 17)
   Chapter-V: Conduct of Arbitral Proceedings (Articles 18 to 27)
   Chapter-VI: Making of Arbitral Award and Termination of Proceedings (Arbitration 28 to 33)
   Chapter-VII: Recourse against Arbitral Award (Article 34)
   Chapter-VIII: Finality and Enforcement of Arbitral Awards (Articles 35 and 36).
4. The bracketed portion was first inserted by Amending Act No. 3 of 2015 w.e.f. 23 October 2015, with a further amendment by Amending Act No. 33 of 2019 (August 2019).
5. 2008 (14) SCC 271.\
6. Remarks of Justice S. B. Sinha in 2008 (14) SCC 271, para 23, page 279:

   "**23.** Section 28 of the 1996 Act is imperative in character in view of Section 2(6) thereof, which excludes the same from those provisions which parties derogate from (if so, provided by the Act). The intention of the legislature appears to be clear that Indian nationals should not be permitted to derogate from Indian law. This is part of the public policy of the country."

7. From the beginning under the Supreme Court Rules "every cause, appeal or matter shall be heard by a Bench consisting of not less than two Judges nominated by the Chief Justice, except a Vacation Judge sitting during the vacation of the Supreme Court of India".
8. *State of West Bengal* vs. *Associated Contractors*: 2015 (1) SCC 32 (3 judges) at para 17, page 436: "The decision of the Chief Justice or his designate, not being the decision of the Supreme Court or the High Court, as the case may be, has no precedential value being a decision of a judicial authority which is not a Court of Record".
9. 2012 (9) SCC 552 (para 28 at page 836).
10. 2016 (10) SCC 813 at para 28.
11. 2016 (2) Arb. L. R. 179 at para 56 (page 203).
12. 2016 (10) SCC 813, para 28.
13. *Sasan Power Ltd.* vs. *North American Coal Corporation India Pvt. Ltd.*, (decided on 11 September 2015, and reported in 2016 (2) Arb. L.R. 179 page 203.
14. The recommended definition in Article 1 of the Model Law reads as follows:

    "Article 1: Scope of application

    1. This law applies to *international commercial arbitration*, subject to any agreement in force between this state and any other state or states.
    2. The provisions of this law, except articles 8, 9, 35 and 36, apply only if the place of arbitration is in the territory of this state.
    3. An arbitration is international if:

(a) the parties to an arbitration agreement have, at the time of the conclusion of that agreement, their places of business in different states; or

(b) one of the following places is situated outside the state in which the parties have their places of business:

(i) the place of arbitration if determined in, or pursuant to, the arbitration agreement;

(ii) any place where a substantial part of the obligations of the commercial relationship is to be performed or the place with which the subject-matter of the dispute is most closely connected; or

(c) *the parties have expressly agreed that the subject-matter of the arbitration agreement relates to more than one country.* (Underling Supplied)

4. For the purposes of paragraph (3) of this article:

(a) if a party has more than one place of business, the place of business is that which has the closest relationship to the arbitration agreement;

(b) if a party does not have a place of business, reference is to be made to his habitual residence.

5. This law shall not affect any other law of this state by virtue of which certain disputes may not be submitted to arbitration or may be submitted to arbitration only according to provisions other than those of this law."

15. MMTC vs. *Sterlite Ltd.* (November 1996) reported in AIR 1997 SC 645

16. Article II (3) of the New York Convention reads:

"II(3). The court of a contracting state, when seized of an action in a matter in respect of which the parties have made an agreement within the meaning of this article, shall, at the request of one of the parties, refer the parties to arbitration, unless it finds that the said agreement is null and void, inoperative or incapable of being performed."

17. *Fibreco Pulp Inc.* vs. *Star Shipping and others* 20.2.1998 affirmed on 20.10.1998: reported in 1998 FCJ No.97 affirmed in 1998 - 156 FTR 127, CLOUT (*Case Law on Uncitral Texts: A legal database of worldwide court decisions and arbitral awards on UNCITRAL texts*).
18. In India this power is presently given to the chief justice of a high court (or to a judge designated by him) to appoint an arbitrator upon failure of parties to agree, and in the case of an "international commercial arbitration" it is the Chief Justice of the Supreme Court of India (or a judge to be designated by him) who exercises the power.
19. In *MMTC* vs. *Sterlite*, AIR 1997 SC 645 it was contended by the Attorney General of India appearing on behalf of the public sector company (MMTC) that the proviso to Section 10(1) of the Act, which stated that the number of arbitrators shall not be an even number rendered all arbitration agreements entered into prior to the commencement of the Act invalid. There were thousands of such agreements pending prior to the coming into force of the Act of 1996. But the Supreme Court of India held that the requirement of the number of arbitrators was not a vital element of the definition of arbitration agreement and the validity of an arbitration agreement did not depend on the number of arbitrators specified. The number of arbitrators was dealt with separately in Section 10 of the Act (a machinery provision for the working of the Arbitration Act). It was held that in respect of arbitration agreements under the 1940 Act (which contemplated appointment of two arbitrators who would appoint an umpire in case they disagree), was in essence an appointment of an uneven number and was valid

and Section 10(2) (on failing the determination referred to in sub-section (1) the Arbitral Tribunal shall consist of a sole arbitrator) was inapplicable. It was held that an arbitration agreement even before the enactment of the new Act was one that would be deemed to be an arbitration providing in essence for three arbitrators (i.e. two arbitrators appointed by each of the parties and an umpire appointed by the arbitrators (or if they could not agree, by the court).

20. In Article 11, the word *court* is used to refer to either a court or any other authority specified in Article 6.
21. The delegate of the Chief Justice of the Supreme Court of India or of the chief justice of a high court has always been a judge of that court.
22. *Till it is brought into force, Section 11, as it obtained under the 1996 Act, as amended by Act No. 3 of 2016, will continue to operate.*
23. Section 11(6A): "The Supreme Court or, as the case may be, the high court, while considering any application under sub-section (4) or sub-section (5) or sub-section (6), shall, notwithstanding any judgment, decree or order of any court, confine to the examination of the existence of an arbitration agreement."
24. Section 11(7): "A decision on a matter entrusted by sub-section (4) or sub-section (5) or sub-section (6) to 3 [the Supreme Court or, as the case may be, the high court or the person or institution designated by such court is final and no appeal including Letters Patent Appeal shall lie against such decision]."
25. Section 11(10): "The Supreme Court or, as the case may be, the high court, may make such scheme as the said court may deem appropriate for dealing with matters entrusted by sub-section (4) or sub-section (5) or sub-section (6), to it.]"
26. *The re-amended new Section 11, will be brought into force on such date/dates as the Central Government appoints*—which, of course, will be only after the Arbitration Council of India

(under Part-IA), has been constituted and its duties and functions have been designated.

27. First Working Group Report, A/CN. 9/216 para 43
28. See First Secretariat Note, A/CN. 9/207, para 65
29. Holtzmann and Neuhaus: *A Guide to the UNICTRAL Model Law on International Commercial Arbitration* (*Legislative History and Commentray*), Kluwer Law and Taxation Publishers, Netherlands, 1995, at Pp. 478-480.
30. Article 6 provides for each state enacting that the Model Law should specify the court/courts competent to exercise the functions referred to in Articles 11(3), 11(4), 13(3), 14, 16, 16(3) and 34(2) of the Model Law.
31. Thomas H. Webster: *Handbook of UNCITRAL Arbitration—Commentary, Precedents & Models for UNCITRAL-based Arbitration Rules*, 2nd Edition, Sweet & Maxwell, UK, 2014, Pp. 391-392.
32. The words "at any times after the making of the arbitral award but before it is enforceable in accordance with Section 30", in Section 17 have been omitted by the amendments of July 2019 (Section 4).
33. Omitted words: "or at any time after the making of the arbitral award but before it is enforced in accordance with Section 36."
34. Section 17(2) had been added by the Amending Act No. 3 of 2016, pursuant to a recommendation made in the 246th Report of India's Law Commission.
35. Although the high level committee (in its report of July 2017) had framed "model arbitration rules in an annexure to the report and had recommended with these so called model arbitration rules" should be incorporated in a new sub-section (3) of Section 19. This recommendation does not appear to have been accepted since it does not figure in the Amendment Act of 2019.

36. In this case it was also held that a decision regarding the venue of arbitration proceedings would not be an award or interim award, though the ultimate award could be assailed under Section 34(2) of the Act, if the decision on the question of venue was erroneous.
37. After sub-section (3) of Section 23, which provides that 'unless otherwise agreed by the parties either party may amend or supplement its claim or defence during the course of arbitral proceedings unless the arbitral tribunal considers it inappropriate to allow the amendment or supplement having regard to the delay in making it'.
38. Court assistance in taking evidence.
    1. The arbitral tribunal, or a party with the approval of the arbitral tribunal, may apply to the court for assistance in taking evidence.
    2. The application shall specify:
       (a) the names and addresses of the parties and the arbitrators;
       (b) the general nature of the claim and the relief sought;
       (c) the evidence to be obtained, in particular (i) the name and address of any person to be heard as witness or expert witness and a statement of the subject-matter of the testimony required; (ii) the description of any document to be produced or property to be inspected.
    3. The court may, within its competence and according to its rules on taking evidence, execute the request by ordering that the evidence be provided directly to the arbitral tribunal.
    4. The court may, while making an order under sub-section (3), issue the same processes to witnesses as it may issue in suits tried before it.

5. Persons failing to attend in accordance with such process, or making any other default, or refusing to give their evidence, or guilty of any contempt to the arbitral tribunal during the conduct of arbitral proceedings, shall be subject to the like disadvantages, penalties and punishments by order of the court on the representation of the arbitral tribunal as they would incur for the like offences in suits tried before the court.
4. In this section, the expression "Processes" includes summonses and commissions for the examination of witnesses and summonses to produce documents.

39. The judgment of May 2019 has been reported in 2019 (8) Scale, pages 47 to 92.
40. Cases of actual dead lock have been rare. In the history of the ICC during a period of 60 years, provisions in its rules that allowed the presiding arbitrator to make decisions where there was no majority, has occurred only twice!
41. Section 31A (Regime for Costs) applies only to domestic arbitrations. The recommendations of the High-Level Committee (in its report of July 2017) had recommended a corresponding provision about costs in Part-II as well, but this was not incorporated in the Amending Act No. 33 of 2019.
42. Holtzman & Neuhaus: *A Guide to The UNCITRAL Model Law on International Commercial Arbitration—Legislative History and Commentary, Kluwer Law and Taxation Publishers, Netherlands, 1995, at* p. 837.
43. Levy: *Dissenting Opinions in International Arbitrations in Switzerland,* Vol. 5, Arbitration International, 1989, page 35.
44. Allen Redfren's FRESHFIELD Lecture: 'Dissenting Opinion in International Commercial Arbitrations: The Good, the Bad and the Ugly', *Arbitration International,* Vol. 20, 2004, p. 223.

45. In a recent case (8 May 2019) in *Ssangyong Engineering & Construction Company Ltd.* vs. *National Highways Authority of India* (NHAI) reported in 2019 (8) Scale 41, (a decision of the Supreme Court of India) a Bench of 2 judges set aside the majority opinion in a domestic award of 3 arbitrators. But went on also to hold as follows: [2019 (8) Scale at page 92]:

> "Under the Scheme of Section 34 of the 1996 Act, the disputes that were decided by the majority award would have to be referred afresh to another arbitration. This would cause considerable delay and be contrary to one of the important objectives of the 1996 Act, namely, speedy resolution of disputes by the arbitral process under the Act. *Therefore, in order to do complete justice between the parties, invoking our power under Article 142 of the Constitution of India,* and given the fact that there is a minority award which awards the appellant its claim based upon the formula mentioned in the agreement between the parties, we uphold the minority award, and state that it is this award, together with interest, that will now be executed between the parties."

Article 142(1) of the Constitution of India referred to in the judgment reads as follows:

> "*The Supreme Court in the exercise of its jurisdiction may pass such decree or make such order as is necessary for doing complete justice in any cause or matter pending before it,* and any decree so passed or order so made shall be enforceable throughout the territory of India in such manner as may be prescribed by or under any law made by Parliament and, until provision in that behalf is so made, in such manner as the President may by order prescribe."

46. "32(2)(b) The arbitral tribunal shall issue an order for the termination of the arbitral proceedings where
    (a). . .
    (b) the parties agree on the termination of the proceedings.
    (c) . . ."
47. Holtzman & Neuhaus: *A Guide to The UNCITRAL Model Law on International Commercial Arbitration—Legislative History and Commentary, Kluwer Law and Taxation Publishers, Netherlands, 1995, at* p. 911.
48. Explanations 1 and 2 to Section 34(2)(b) ("the Court finds that the arbitral award is in conflict with the public policy of India") and sub-section (2A) of Section 34 read as follows:

    "Explanation 1. For the avoidance of any doubt, it is clarified that an award is in conflict with the public policy of India, only if,

    the making of the award was induced or affected by fraud or corruption or was in violation of section 75 or section 81; or

    it is in contravention with the fundamental policy of Indian law; or

    it is in conflict with the most basic notions of morality or justice.

    "Explanation 2: For the avoidance of doubt, the test as to whether there is a contravention with the fundamental policy of Indian law, shall not entail a review on the merits of the dispute.

    (2A) An arbitral award arising out of arbitrations other than international commercial arbitrations, may also be set aside by the court, if the court finds that the award is vitiated by patent illegality appearing on the face of the award:

    —provided that an award shall not be set aside merely on the ground of an erroneous application of the law or by reappreciation of evidence."

In the case of *Ssangyong Eng. & Constructions Co. Ltd.* vs. *NHAI* (judgment recently reported in 2019 (8) Scale, page 41 at page 51), the Supreme Court of India held:

> "12. There is no doubt that in the present case, fundamental changes have been made in the law. The expansion of "public policy of India" in *ONGC Ltd.* vs. *Saw Piper Ltd.* (2003) 5 SCC 705 ["Saw Pipe"] and *ONGC Ltd.* vs. *Western Geco International Ltd.* (2014) 9 SCC 263 ["Western Gecco"] has been done away with, and a new ground of "patent illegality", with inbuilt exceptions, has been introduced. Given this, we declare that Section 34, as amended, will apply only to Section 34 applications that have been made to the court on or after 23.10.2015, irrespective of the fact that the arbitration proceedings may have commenced prior to that date".

49. Available at: http://legalaffairs.gov.in/sites/default/files/Report-HLC.pdf
50. Despite the recommendations of the High Level Committee (Report of July 2017) that a corresponding provision for expeditious disposal of arbitrators abroad be also applied to New York Convention Awards (by insertion of sub-section 4) in Section 48); this recommendation was not accepted and does not find a place in Amending Act No. 33 of 2019.
51. Presumably on the basis of a higher law—the Constitution of India—in which Article 141 provides that the law declared by the Supreme Court of India "shall be binding on all courts within the territory of India".
52. *Oil Natural Gas Corporation Ltd.* vs. *SAW Pipes Ltd.*, (2003) 5 SCC 705- (Sections 34(2)(a)(v) and 34(2)(b)); *The Security Printing and Minting Corporation of India Limited and Ors.* vs. *Gandhi Industrial Corporation*, (2007) 13 SCC 236

(34(2)(b)(ii); *ONGC Ltd.* vs. *Garware Shipping Corpn. Ltd.*, (2007) 13 SCC 434 (Section 34) [judgment does not refer to the particular clause of Section 34]; *Delhi Development Authority* vs. *R.S. Sharma and Co., New Delhi*, (2008) 13 SCC 80 (Section 34(2).

53. *Narayan Prasad Lohia* vs. *Nikunj Kumar Lohia and Ors.*, (2002) 3 SCC 572- (Section 34(2)(a)(v); *Tata Hydro Electric Power Supply Co. Ltd. and Ors.* vs. *Union of India*, (2003) 4 SCC 172 (Section 34) [judgment does not refer to the particular clause of section 34 while reversing the decision of the high court]; *M. Anasuya Devi* vs. *M. Manik Reddy* 2003 (8) SCC 565 (section 34) (high court judgment set-aside and case remitted to); *Hindustan Zinc Ltd.* vs. *Friends Coal Carbonisation*, (2006) 4 SCC 445 (Section 34(2)(b)) (Trial Court judgment restored); *Mc Dermott International Inc.* vs. *Burn Standard Co. Ltd.* 2006 (11) SCC 181=2006 (2) Arb. LR 498; *Venture Global Engineering* vs. *Satyam Computer Services Ltd.* 2008 (4) SCC 190; and 2010 (8) SCC 660 section 341(2) (International Commercial Award (London). The Supreme Court set aside the high court and the trial court orders and remitted award for reconsideration; *Bharat Drilling and Foundation Treatment Pvt. Ltd* vs. *State of Jharkhand* 2009 (16) SCC 705. (section 34(2); *State of Goa* vs. *Praveen Enterprises*, AIR 2011 SC 3814 (Section 34: Judgment does not refer to the particular clause of section 34 part of the award which had been set aside by the high court, was upheld by the Supreme Court; *J. G. Engineers Pvt. Ltd.* vs. *Union of India (UOI) and Ors.*, 2011 (5) SCC 758=AIR 2011 SC 2477 (Section 34(2)(a)(iv) and 34(2)(b)(ii)); *Leela Hotels Ltd.* vs. *Housing and Urban Development Corporation Ltd.* AIR 2012 SC 903 (Section 34) [judgment does not refer to the particular clause of section 34]; *Associate Builders* vs. *Delhi Development Authority* (2015) 3 SCC 49 (Section 32(2)(b)(ii) and 34(2)(a)(iii); *Sri Chittaranjan*

Maity vs *Union of India* AIR 2017 SC 4588; Appeal partly allowed (Section 11(6), 34 and 31). (The Supreme Court of India partially allowed the appeal to the extent of the interest being made payable); *Sutlej Construction Limited* vs *Union Territory of Chandigarh* 2018 1 SCC 718. (Section 34); *Ssangyong Engineering and Construction Co. Ltd.* vs *National Highways Authority of India* (*NHAI*) (2019 SCC OnLine SC 677) 2019 (8) Scale 41 (Section 34(2)(a)(i)-(iv) (majority award which was also upheld by the high court was set aside and minority award was directed by the Supreme Court as the award to be executed; *Parsa Kente Collieries Ltd.* vs. *Rajasthan Rajya Vidyut Utpadan Nigam Ltd.* 2019 (8) Scale 434 (Section 34(2) and section 37).

54. *Olympus Superstructures Pvt. Ltd.* vs. *Meena Vijay Khetan and Ors.*, (1999) 5 SCC 651 (Section 34(2)(b)(i)); *Satyanarayana Construction Co.* vs. *Union of India* (2011) 15 SCC 101 (Section 34) [The high court judgment (reported in 2005 (2) Arb. LR 496 modifying the award and the same was upheld by the Supreme Court]; *Shipping Corporation of India Ltd.* vs. *Mare Shipping Inc.* AIR 2011 SC 2608 (Section 34); *P. R. Shah, Shares and Stockbroker (P) Ltd.* vs. *B. H. H. Securities (P) Ltd. and Ors.* AIR 2012 SC 1866 (Section 34); *ONGC* vs. *Western Geco International* 2014 (9) SCC 363 (Section 34(2)(b)(ii)) (award modified); *Navodaya Mass Entertainment Ltd.* vs. *J. M. Combines* (2015) 5 SCC 698 (Section 34); *Swan Gold Mining Ltd.* vs. *Hindustan Copper Ltd.* (2015) 5 SCC 739—(Section 34(2)(b)(ii); *State of Orissa* vs. *Samantary Construction* 2015 SCC Online SC 856 (Section 34(2)(b)(ii)) [upheld partially by the Supreme Court to the extent of the amount of the award] 2007 (2) Arb. LR 309 (Orissa); *State of West Bengal* vs. *Associated Contractors* AIR 2015 SC 260 (Section 34); *Harsha Constructions* vs. *Union of India* AIR 2015 SC 270—Section 34(2)(a)(iv) [The Supreme Court partially upheld the award]; *National Highways Authority of India* vs. *JSC Centrodorstroy* (2016) 12 SCC 592 (Section 34); *Union of India* Vs *Susaka Pvt. Ltd. And Ors.* AIR 2017 SC 5721. (Section 34 and 31(7)(a) and (b); *Maharashtra State Electricity Distribution Company Ltd.* vs *Datar Switchgear Limited and Ors.* AIR 2018 SC 529 (Section 34(2)(a)(iv); *MMTC Ltd.* vs. *Vedanta Ltd.* AIR 2019 SC 1168 (Sections 34(b)(2)(ii) and 37).

55. Article 36—Grounds for refusing recognition or enforcement.
56. By the Arbitration and Conciliation (Amendment) Act No. 33 of 2019, Section 37(1) for the words "An appeal", the words, "Notwithstanding anything contained in any other law for the time being in force, an appeal" have been substituted.
57. These provisions in Section 42A and Section 42B are in conformity with the 2006 Revision of the UNCITRAL Model Law, 1985 effective from 2010 (Article XVI of the Revised Rules for Arbitrators Immunity). The UNCITRAL Arbitration Rules 1976, initially did not provide any immunity for arbitrators, but the new Article XVI in the 2006 Revision of the Rules of the UNCITRAL Arbitration Rules has provided for a broad exclusion of liability that covered even gross negligence, whilst maintaining potential liability for intentional wrongdoing. Despite the risk that such a broad exclusion of liability might not be recognised in some jurisdictions, the Working Group of UNCITRAL deliberately granted the protection that was contained in Article XVI (in the year 2006: but effective from 2010).
58. At page 9 of one of the early commentaries on the Arbitration and Conciliation Act No. 26 of 1996 by P. Chandrasekhara Rao, Law Secretary, Government of India, (1997 Edition), and principal draftsman of the Bill which was passed by India's Parliament as Act 26 of 1996, it was stated:

"While drafting the Act the International Commercial Arbitration Act, 1986 of British Columbia was taken as a model for it conforms largely to the Indian drafting style. Though the drafting style of the Act differs from that of the Model Law, the Act retains the language of the Model Law to the extent possible."

59. Dr Peter Binder's Fourth Edition (2019) of International Commercial Arbitration and Mediation in UNCITRAL Model Law Jurisdictions published by Wolters Kluwer, Netherlands—has given various references and citations of court decisions around the world reported in CLOUT (Case Law on UNCITRAL Text available at: (http://www.uncitral.org/clout)) for each and every Article (Article 1 to 36) of the UNCITRAL Model Law—in respect of which the corresponding Sections of India's 1996 Act (as amended) are Sections 2 to 36.

5

Work-In-Progress

The Arbitration Council of India[1] and The New Delhi International Arbitration Centre[2]

Setting up the Arbitration Council of India and New Delhi International Arbitration Centre:

Under the 1996 Act no provision was made for promoting institutional arbitration in India as was done in Singapore[3] and in Hong Kong[4].

In December 2016, a high-level committee was constituted[5] by the Government of India to review the institutionalisation of arbitration mechanism in the country and to improve the overall quality and performance of over 35 arbitral institutions functioning in the country, as also to encourage India becoming a seat of arbitration. The high-level committee made the following recommendations in its report of July 2017[6]:

- In Part-I of the report ("Institutional Arbitration in India") it was suggested that Part-IA—"Arbitration Council of India"—be added in the 1996 Act, setting out its composition and functions.

- In Part-II of the report—"The International Centre for Alternative Dispute Resolution"—ICADR—it was recommended that since an arbitral institution (ICADR), funded by the government already existed, but had not achieved the objectives with which it was setup in 1995, the Government of India should take it over, vest it in the New Delhi International

Arbitration Centre for creating an independent and autonomous regime for institutional arbitration.

- In Part-III of the report—"Bilateral Investment Treaty Arbitrations"—suitable measures were recommended for reform in the dispute management and dispute resolution under Bilateral Investment Treaty Arbitrations.

The Government of India accepted the recommendations of the high-level committee report made in Part-I of the Report and introduced in Parliament the Arbitration and Conciliation (Amendment) Bill No. 21 of 2019, to amend the 1996 Act. The objects and reasons of the Bill[7] stated inter-alia as follows:

> "4. The High-Level Committee submitted its Report on 30th July 2017. With a view to strengthen institutional arbitration in the country, the said committee, inter alia, recommended for the establishment of an independent body for grading of arbitral institutions and accreditation of arbitrators, etc. The committee has also recommended certain amendments to the said Act to minimise the need to approach the courts for appointment of arbitrators. After examination of the said recommendations, with a view to make India a hub of institutional arbitration for both domestic and international arbitration, it was decided (once again) to amend the Arbitration and Conciliation Act, 1996.
>
> 5 . . .

6. The salient features of the Arbitration and Conciliation (Amendment) Bill, 2019, inter alia, are as follows:

(i) to amend Section 11 of the Act relating to "Appointment of Arbitrators" so as to change the present system of appointment of arbitrators, by the Chief Justice of the Supreme Court in the case of International Commercial Arbitration, and the Chief Justice of the High Courts in all other cases by delegating its power to appoint arbitrators to a judge in the court) or high court, to a system where the arbitrators shall be appointed by the "arbitral institutions" designated by the Supreme Court or High Court;
(ii) in case where no graded arbitral institutions are available, the Chief Justice of the concerned High Court may maintain a panel of arbitrators for discharging the functions and duties of arbitral institutions;
(iii) to insert a new Part 1A to the (1996) Act, for the establishment and incorporation of an independent body namely, the Arbitration Council of India for the purpose of grading of arbitral institutions and accreditation of arbitrators, etc.;
(iv) to amend Section 23 of the Act relating to "Statement of claim and defence" so as to provide that the statement of claim and defence shall be completed within a period of six months from the date the arbitrator receives the notice of appointment;
(v) to provide that the arbitrator, the arbitral institutions

and the parties shall maintain confidentiality of information relating to arbitral proceedings and also protect the arbitrator or arbitrators from any suit or other legal proceedings for any action or omission done in good faith in the course of arbitration proceedings (by adding two additional sections); and

(vi) to clarify that Section 26 of the Arbitration and Conciliation (Amendment) Act, 2015[8], is applicable only to the arbitral proceedings which commenced on or after 23rd October 2015, and to such court proceedings which emanate from such arbitral proceedings."

The Arbitration and Conciliation (Amendment) Bill No. XXI of 2019, was ultimately passed by both Houses of Parliament in the very first session of the 17th Lok Sabha (constituted after the General Elections), in July 2019. After the Bill was approved by the Council of States, and received presidential assent, it was titled: "The Arbitration and Conciliation (Amendment) Act No. 33 of 2019"[9].

The Act has incorporated Part-IA (after Part-I) in the 1996 Act providing for the establishment, composition and functions of the "Arbitration Council Of India" as under:

- *Section* 43B deals with establishment and incorporation of the Arbitration Council of India, with its head office in Delhi;

- *Section* 43C deals with the composition of the Arbitration Council. It is to consist of the following members:

(i) a chairperson (who is a former judge of the Supreme Court or chief justice or a judge of high court or an eminent person, appointed by the Government of India in consultation with the Chief Justice of India);

(ii) an eminent arbitration practitioner nominated by the Government of India and

(iii) an eminent academician also appointed by the Government of India in consultation with the chairperson;

(iv) and the following exoffico members, viz. Secretary of the Ministry of Law, Secretary of Ministry of Finance of (GOI), and one representative (as part-time member) of a recognised body of commerce and industry (on rotation basis) to be chosen by the Government of India and as well as a chief executive officer as a Member-Secretary.

Section 43D, lays down duties and functions of the Arbitration Council of India including the power to review the grading of arbitral institutions as well as of the arbitrators.

The Arbitration and Conciliation (Amending) Act No. 33 of 2019, also amended and added several sections in Part-I[10]

The amendments affected in July 2019, have also added a new *Section* 87—after Section 86 of the principal 1996 Act—stating that the amendments made to the 1996 Act, by the Arbitration and Conciliation (Amendment) Act

No.3 of 2016 apply only prospectively. This section is quoted in the endnote.[11]

The Amending Act No. 33 of 2019, also includes in Part-IA the further provisions relating to "Arbitration Council of India" as under:

- Section 43A (deals with definitions of "Chairperson", "Council" and "Member";

- Section 43E provides that vacancies, defects in appointments or any irregularity in the procedure are not to invalidate proceedings of the Arbitration Council;

- Section 43F provides the method of resignation of members of the Arbitration Council;

- Section 43G provides for grounds on which a member can be removed by the Government of India;

- Section 43H provides that the Arbitration Council may appoint experts and constitute such committees of experts to discharge functions as may be specified by the regulations;

- Section 43I provides for the criteria of grading arbitral institutions by the Arbitration Council.

The above changes are linked to the now amended Section 11(3A) as being the pre-July 2019 system of appointing arbitrators by the Supreme Court or a High

Court, to a system where the arbitrators are to be appointed by the arbitral institution as designated by the Supreme Court of India or the High Court—arbitral institutions having been graded by the Arbitration Council of India; (one of its original functions).

- Section 43J, along with a newly added Eighth Schedule, provides the norms for accreditation of arbitrators i.e. qualifications and experience of arbitrator specified in the Eighth Schedule;

- Section 43K provides that the Arbitration Council of India will maintain an electronic depository of arbitral awards made in India;

- Section 43L provides the Arbitration Council with the power to make regulations in consultation with the Government of India;

- Section 43M deals with the qualification, appointment and other conditions of service of the Chief Executive Officer of the Council who is to be responsible for the day-to-day administration of the Arbitration Council of India.[12]

Pursuant to the recommendations of the high-level committee in Part-II of its report, the Government of India having accepted the same resolved to pass a separate law by introducing "The New Delhi International Arbitration Centre Bill No. 127 of 2019". As mentioned above, the Bill was passed by Parliament and received the Presidential assent in July 2019 to become "the New Delhi International Arbitration Centre Act No: 17 of 2019.[13] Its Statement of Objects and Reasons inter-alia reads as under:

> "1. The dispute resolution process has a huge impact on the economy and doing business in our country. The rapidly changing economic activity demands expeditious settlement of disputes, creation and establishment of mechanism such as institutional arbitration. This is necessary to inspire confidence and credibility among the litigants of commercial disputes. The huge pendency of cases in courts further underlines the need for strengthening the Alternative Dispute Resolution mechanism.
>
> 2. With a view to promote institutional arbitration and to make India a hub of international arbitration, a high level committee headed by Justice B. N. Srikrishna, former judge, Supreme Court of India, was constituted, inter alia, to identify the roadblocks in the development of institutional arbitration, examine specific issues affecting the Indian arbitration landscape and prepare a roadmap for making India a robust centre for international and domestic arbitration.
>
> 3. The committee, inter alia, recommended that the International Centre for Alternative Dispute Resolution, which was set up in the year 1995, with the government funds to promote alternative dispute resolution mechanism has however not been able to achieve the objectives for which it had been set up. The committee further recommended

that International Centre for Alternative Dispute Resolution should be taken over with complete revamp of its governance structure to include only experts of repute who can lend credibility and respectability to the institution and be re-branded as a centre of national importance to highlight its character as a flagship arbitral institution.

4. In view of the above, it has been decided to establish a new institution to be called the New Delhi International Arbitration Centre for better management of arbitration in the country and to declare it as an institution of national importance. Further, the undertakings of the International Centre for Alternative Dispute Resolution needs to be taken over without interfering with its activities and without adversely affecting the character of it as a society, so that the existing infrastructure and other facilities which have been set up with the public funds provided by the government may be appropriately utilised by the NDIAC (New Delhi International Arbitration Centre) for the overall development of institutional arbitration.
5. . . .
6. The Bill envisaged appointment of persons of repute and having knowledge and expertise in institutional arbitration as chairperson and members of the New Delhi International Arbitration Centre. The objects of the Centre was to bring targeted reforms to develop it as a flagship institution for domestic and international arbitration and to conduct arbitration in a professional manner in a cost-effective way. The

Bill also proposed to set up an arbitration chamber, which would empanel reputed arbitrators at national and international level. An Arbitration Academy was also proposed to be set up by New Delhi International Arbitration Centre to train arbitrators in India, so as to empower them to compete on par with reputed international arbitral institutions.

7. As the Bill was pending for consideration in the Rajya Sabha, in the interest of promotion of institutional arbitration, it had become expedient to take over the undertakings of the International Centre for Alternative Dispute Resolution including its regional offices and vest the same in the Central Government before it got finally vested in the New Delhi International Arbitration Centre. The New Delhi International Arbitration Centre was declared as an institution of national importance for its overall development as an arbitration hub for promoting quick and efficient dispute resolution."

By this NDIAC Act No: 17 of 2019, "The New Delhi International Arbitration Centre" (briefly called the "Centre") has been established to create an independent and autonomous regime for institutionalised arbitration and (hopefully) for the better management of arbitration so as to make it a hub for institutional arbitration.

The composition of the "Centre" as prescribed (under Section 5) consists of:

(i) a chairperson, who may be a judge of the Supreme Court or a high court, or an eminent person with special knowledge and experience in the conduct or administration of arbitration;

(ii) two eminent persons having substantial knowledge and experience in institutional arbitration (full-time or part-time members);

(iii) one representative of a recognized body of commerce and industry (on rotational basis) by Central Government (part-time member);

(iv) Secretary, Ministry of Law and Justice (ex-officio member);

(v) one financial adviser nominated by the Ministry of Finance (ex-officio member); and

(vi) a chief executive officer (ex-officio-member), responsible for the day-to-day administration of the Centre.

The "Centre" is entrusted with the following objectives (under Section 14) namely:

(i) promote research, provide training and organise conferences and seminars in alternative dispute resolution matters;

(ii) provide facilities and administrative assistance for the conduct of arbitration, mediation and conciliation proceedings;

(iii) maintain a panel of accredited professionals to conduct arbitration, mediation and conciliation proceedings.

And the "Centre" is also entrusted with the following functions (under Section 15) namely:

(i) facilitating conduct of arbitration and conciliation in a professional, timely and cost-effective manner; and

(ii) promoting studies in the field of alternative dispute resolution.

The "Centre" is expected (once again, hopefully) to establish a Chamber of Arbitration (under Section 28) which would maintain a permanent panel of reputed arbitrators.

It is also empowered to establish an Arbitration Academy (under Section 29) for training arbitrators and conducting research in the area of alternative dispute resolution and may constitute other committees to administer its functions.

As regards the recommendations of the high-level committee report in Part-III (of the Report)—"the Bilateral Investment Treaty Arbitrations"—no decision has been taken as yet by the Government of India.

End Notes:

1. Inserted by Part-IA (Section 43A to 43M) of the Arbitration and Conciliation (Amendment) Act No. 33 of 2019.
2. Set up by the New Delhi International Arbitration Centre Act No: 17 of 2019.
3. In Singapore, the SIAC is the default appointing authority under the International Arbitration Act 1994 (Section 9A(2) read with Section 2(1) and 8(2))
4. In Hongkong, under the Arbitration Ordinance 2011, the Hongkong International Arbitration Centre has been

designated as the appointing authority for arbitrators where parties cannot appoint arbitrators (Section 24(3) and (4) read with Section 13(2) of Arbitration Ordinance 2011).

5. Under the Chairmanship of Justice B. N. Srikrishna, retired Supreme Court Judge, it gave its report in July 2017, and is available on http://legalaffairs.gov.in/sites/default/files/Report-HLC.pdf)
6. Available at http://legalaffairs.gov.in/sites/default/files/Report-HLC.pdf
7. http://164.100.47.4/BillsTexts/RSBillTexts/asintroduced/Arbitration-Rs%20intro-E-15719.pdf A Statement of Objects and Reasons is invariably attached to every Bill in Parliament in either the Lok Sabha or in the Upper House (Rajya Sabha).
8. Which had been introduced pursuant to 246th Report of Law Commission of India (2014)
9. http://egazette.nic.in/WriteReadData/2019/210414.pdf
10. For instance: in Section 2 (inserted sub-section (ca), (i & j); in Section 11 it inserted sub-clause (3A), and also amended sub-clauses (4), (5), (6), (8), (9), and amended clauses (11 to 14); of Section 11; amended Section 17 and inserted sub-section (4) in Section 23; and in Section 29A(1) it amended sub-section (1) and inserted a proviso to sub-section (4); it amended in sub-section 2(a) in Section 34; it amended sub-section (1) of Section 37; and added new Sections 42A, and 42B; it amended Section 45 as well as Section 50; and added a new Section 87 as well as the Eighth Schedule.
11. "87.Unless the parties otherwise agree, the amendments made to this Act by the Arbitration and Conciliation (Amendment) Act, 2015 shall
    (a) not apply to:
        (i) arbitral proceedings commenced before the commencement of the Arbitration and Conciliation (Amendment) Act, 2015;

(ii) court proceedings arising out of or in relation to such arbitral proceedings irrespective of whether such court proceedings are commenced prior to or after the commencement of the Arbitration and Conciliation (Amendment) Act, 2015;

(b) apply only to arbitral proceedings commenced on or after the commencement of the Arbitration and Conciliation (Amendment) Act, 2015 and to court proceedings arising out of or in relation to such arbitral proceedings." (See the criticism of this section in 2018 (6) SCC 287).

12. The Arbitration and Conciliation (Amendment) Act, 2019, is to come into force "on such date as the Central Government may by notification in the official gazette appoint for different provisions of the Act, and any reference in any such provision to the commencement of the Act shall be construed as a reference to the coming into force of that provision (Section 1(2) of the Amending Act No: 33 of 2019).

13. https://www.greengazette.in/notices/the-new-delhi-international-arbitration-centre-act-2019_20190726-210-00036-00000

6

Enforcement of Foreign Awards

Made by Arbitral Bodies/Tribunals

Part-II: CHAPTER-I

Chapter I—New York Convention Awards (Sections 44 To 52)—in Part-II of the Act, applies to New York Convention awards since India was one of the original signatories to the New York Convention 1958.

The New York Convention 1958 only defines the term 'arbitral awards' in Article I (2) as including "not only awards made by arbitrators appointed for each case but also those made by permanent arbitral bodies to which the parties have submitted".

***

The first provision in Chapter I of Part-II is Section 44—the definition section[1]—which defines a '*foreign award*':

> ". . . an arbitral award on differences between persons arising out of legal relationships whether contractual or not, considered as commercial[2] under the law in force in India, made on or after 11.10.1960:
>
> (a) in pursuance to an agreement in writing for arbitration to which the New York Convention (set forth in the First Schedule of the Act) applies, and
>
> (b) in one of such territories as the Central Government, being satisfied that reciprocal provisions have been made, may by notification in the official gazette, declare to be territories to which the said Convention applies."

This chapter does not apply to awards made in countries that are not parties to the New York Convention, although such awards may attract the "Savings" clause in Chapter-I, Part-II of the 1996 Act.[3]

But, when considering whether Chapter I of Part-II of the Act ("New York Convention Awards") applies in a particular case, the provisions of Section 44(b) must always be kept in mind. Not only should the other state or territory be a party to the New York Convention, but in addition a further condition (imposed by Section 44[b]) has also to be satisfied viz. that the Central Government has declared by notification in the official gazette that the other state party to the New York Convention is a "territory to which the Convention applies".

Apart from India, which has been a party to the New York Convention 1958 from its inception, there are a large number of other countries and territories which are also parties to the New York Convention. They now total 161 countries/territories: Papua New Guinea being the 160th (24th July 2019) and the Maldives the 161st (17th September 2019) state party to join the Convention on the Recognition and Enforcement of Foreign Arbitral Awards (the "New York Convention") following others in the South Pacific Region such as Cook Islands, Fiji, and Marshall Islands. (The New York Convention enters into force for Papua New Guinea on 15 October 2019).

Care must be taken to see whether reciprocal provisions have been made[4] (by the Government of India) by notification in the official gazette declaring those territories (states) to be territories (states) to which the Convention applies: a difficult task. In *Swiss Singapore* vs. *M. V. African*

Traders a reference to arbitration under Section 45 (Part-II) of the Act was refused by the High Court of Gujarat (in its judgment dated 7 February 2005) since, though South Africa was a party to the New York Convention 1958, there was no notification by the Government of India in respect of South Africa in the official gazette. Hence, an award made in Durban (South Africa) could not be enforced in India. A summary of this decision is in the *ICCA Yearbook* Vol. XXXV, 2010, at pages 398-400.

So far as India is concerned, at least 97 party states to the New York Convention are (at present) *non-reciprocating territories/states* (i.e. there being no notification in respect of these states/territories under Section 44(b). Hence, Chapter-I of Part-II of the 1996 Act, will not be applicable to "foreign awards" made in these non-reciprocatory territories/states.

At present there are only 64 countries (who are parties to the New York Convention) in respect of which notifications have been so far issued by the Government of India. They include countries/territories also previously notified under the Foreign Awards (Recognition and Enforcement) Act, 1961—an Act now repealed by the 1996 Act.

These 64 countries (in alphabetical order) are: Armenia; Australia (including Australian Antarctic Territory, Christmas Island, Cocos (Keeling) Islands and Norfolk Island), Austria, Azerbaijan, Belarus, Belgium, Botswana, Bulgaria, Canada, Central African Republic, Chile, China (including Hong Kong), Cuba, Czech Republic, Denmark (Faeroe Islands, Greenland), Ecuador, Estonia, Finland, France (Comoro Islands, French Polynesia, New Caledonia, St. Pierre et Miquelon, Wallis and Futuna Island), Federal

Republic of Germany, Georgia, Ghana, Greece, Hungary, Italy, Japan, Kazakhstan, Kuwait, Kyrgyzstan, Latvia, Lithuania, Moldova, Mauritius, Malagasy Republic (Madagascar), Malaysia, Mexico, Morocco, Nigeria, Norway, Philippines, Poland, Republic of Ireland, Republic of Korea, Romania, Russian Federation, San Marino, Singapore, Slovakia, Spain, Sweden, Switzerland, Syrian Arab Republic, Tajikistan, Thailand, The Arab Republic of Egypt, The Netherlands, Trinidad and Tobago, Tunisia, Ukraine, United Kingdom(including Cayman Islands, British, Virgin Islands, Belize, Bermuda, Gibraltar, Guernsey, Isle of Man, Jersey), United Republic of Tanzania, USA(including Canton Islands, American Samoa, Enderby Islands, Guam, Puerto Rico, Virgin Island, Wake Island), Uzbekistan.

***

The next provision in Chapter I of Part-II is Section 45[5] ("Power of Judicial Authority to refer parties to Arbitration"). It incorporates the essence of Clause 3 of Article II of the New York Convention which reads:

> "Article II
>
> . . .
>
> . . . The court of a contracting state, when seized of an action in a matter in respect of which the parties have made an agreement within the meaning of this article, shall, at the request of one of the parties, refer the parties to arbitration, unless it finds that the said

agreement is null and void, inoperative or incapable of being performed."

In Section 45, (corresponding to Article-II (3) of the New York Convention), the only grounds for refusing to refer parties to arbitration are:

> "... that the said agreement is null and void, inoperative or incapable of being performed."

In an article titled "The New York Convention 1958—An Overview" (published on the website of ICCA),[6] Prof. Albert Jan van den Berg (General Editor of the *ICCA Yearbook*) has offered a meaning to these expressions:

> "The words "null and void" may be interpreted as referring to those cases where the arbitration agreement is affected by some invalidity right from the beginning, such as lack of consent due to misrepresentation, duress, fraud or undue influence."

The word "inoperative", says van den Berg, can be said to cover those cases where the arbitration agreement has ceased to have effect, such as revocation by the parties. And as far the words "incapable of being performed" are concerned, they:

> ". . . would seem to apply to those cases where the arbitration cannot be effectively set into motion. . . This may happen where the arbitration clause is too vaguely worded, or other terms of the contract contradict the

parties' intention to arbitrate, as in the case of the so-called co-equal-forum selection clauses. But even in these cases, the courts have interpreted the contract provisions in favour of arbitration."

In the book: *Recognition and Conferment of Foreign Arbitral Awards: A Global Commentary on the New York Convention* by Kronke, Nacimiento, et al. (ed.) (2010), at page 82, it has been stated:

"Most authorities hold that the same schools of thought and approaches regarding the term 'null and void' also apply to the terms 'inoperative' and 'incapable of being performed'. Consequently, the majority of authorities do not interpret these terms uniformly, resulting in an unfortunate lack of uniformity. With that caveat, *we shall give an overview of typical examples where arbitration agreements were held to be (or not to be) inoperative or incapable of being performed.*

The term 'inoperative' refers to cases where the arbitration agreement has ceased to have effect by the time the court is asked to refer the parties to arbitration. For example, the arbitration agreement ceases to have effect if there has already been an arbitral award or a court decision with res judicata effect concerning the same subject matter and parties. (However, the mere existence of multiple proceedings is not sufficient to render the arbitration agreement inoperative). Additionally, the arbitration agreement can cease to have effect if the time limit for initiating the arbitration or rendering the award has expired, provided that it was the parties' intent no longer to be bound by the arbitration agreement due to the expiration of this time limit.

Finally, several authorities have held that the arbitration agreement ceases to have effect if the parties waive arbitration. There are many possible ways of waiving a right to arbitrate. Most commonly, a party will waive the right to arbitrate if, in a court proceeding, it fails to properly invoke the arbitration agreement or if it actively pursues (in Court) claims covered by the arbitration agreement."

In the case of *McDonald's Pvt. Ltd.* vs. *Vikram Bakshi & Co*, reported in 2016 (4) *Arbitration Law Reporter* 250, at page 253, the High Court of Delhi held:

"One of the meanings of the expression *null and void* which was considered by the Supreme Court, (in the case of World Sport Group (Mauritius) 2014 (1) Arb. L. R. 197 SC = 2014 11 SCC 639), was where the arbitration agreement is affected by some invalidity right from the beginning, such as lack of consent due to misrepresentation, duress, fraud or undue influence. This is clearly not the case in the present proceedings. Insofar as the word *inoperative* is concerned, it is said to cover those cases where the arbitration agreement has ceased to have effect, such as the case of revocation by the parties. Another instance of the agreement having become inoperative is where it ceases to have effect because an arbitral award has already been made or there is a court decision with res judicata effect concerning the same subject matter and parties but, it has been expressed that the mere existence of multiple proceedings is not sufficient to render the arbitration agreement inoperative. Thus, the mere existence of the proceedings before the Company Law Board would not amount to rendering the arbitration agreement as being inoperative."

In *McDonald's* case it was also held, following the decision of the Chancery Division of the UK High Court, in *Albon* vs. *Naza Motor Trading Company* (reported in 2007 (2) All E. R. 1075), that the words 'null and void' in the context in which all the words "null and void inoperative or incapable of being performed" occur, mean "devoid of legal effect".

As regards the words 'null and void' the High Court of Madras has pointed out that under the Contract Act, 1872, there are two types of nullity and voidity that are contemplated:

(i) agreements which are unenforceable and of no legal effect right from the inception, which are termed *void ab initio*; and
(ii) agreements which might be valid at the inception, but which become void on account of something that made them unenforceable after inception.

As for the words *'incapable of being performed'* the same High Court (of Madras) has held that one of the facets of 'incapability of being performed' was where a contract was frustrated, and that the word 'inoperative', indicated 'something which has become a dead-letter'; or where the dispute arising out of the underlying contract has been already resolved. This was so held relying on a judgment of the Supreme Court of New South Wales (Australia), an extract of which is reported in the *ICCA Yearbook*, Vol. XXII (1997), at page 609.[7]

A summary of the cases under Section 45, decided by the Supreme Court of India, is set out below:

- In *Owners and Parties interested in the Vessel MV Baltic Confidence* vs. *State Trading Corp of India*, reported in 2001 (7) SCC 473 (2J), the question was whether parties had agreed that the Arbitration Clause in a Charter Party Agreement was applicable to disputes under the Bill of Lading. Citing a large number of English and Indian cases, the Supreme Court of India ruled:

  > "If, on a construction of the arbitration clause of the Charter Party Agreement incorporated in the Bill of Lading, it does not lead to inconsistency or insensibility or absurdity, then effect should be given to the intention of the parties and the arbitration clause as agreed should be made binding on parties to the Bill of Lading."

- In *Shin-Etsu Chemicals* vs. *Aksh Optifibre Ltd.*, reported in 2005 (7) SCC 234 (3J), the question that arose before the Supreme Court was as to the nature of the adjudication that was contemplated by Section 45 of the Arbitration and Conciliation Act, 1996 when an objection was raised about the agreement being "null and void, inoperative or incapable of being performed". It was held, by majority (2:1), that the determination under Section 45 had to be prima facie (and not a final determination).[8] It was thought that a prime facie review of the arbitration agreement would enable arbitrators to decide the question without avoidable interference from judicial authorities, and also ensure a fair opportunity to parties to contest the award after a full hearing.[9]

- *Shakti Bhog Foods Ltd.* vs. *Kola Shipping Ltd.*, 2009 (2) SCC 134 (2J), was a case of a charter–party agreement, and the Supreme Court of India refused to interfere with concurrent findings of fact (recorded by the Trial Court and by the High Court of Andhra Pradesh), holding that although the provisions of Section 45 of the Act applied to a charter-party agreement, there was no reason to accept that the particular agreement in it was "null and void, or inoperative, or incapable of being performed". The Court asserted that the alleged non-existence of the agreement (the Court said) could be raised by the party before the arbitral tribunal in London.
- In *Chloro Controls India Private Limited* vs. *Severn Trent Water Purification Inc.* 2013 (1) SCC 641 (3J), the question was that where several agreements were signed between different parties, some of which contained an arbitration clause, whilst others did not, (the parties being common), a reference of disputes to arbitration could be made under Section 45. The answer of the court was in the affirmative

particularly because the parties to the action were those claiming under, or through parties to the arbitration agreement. It was held that the expression "person claiming through or under" in Section 45, takes within its ambit multi-party agreements and even non-signatory parties.

- In *Enercon (India) Ltd.* vs. *Enercon Gmbh*, 2014 (5) SCC 1 (2J) the Supreme Court had stressed that since an arbitration clause is treated as an agreement independent of the underlying contract, the mere fact that the underlying contract may not be concluded did not justify the court holding the arbitration clause to be "null and void, inoperative or incapable of being performed". It was said:

  "The arbitration clause in the present case provided for the arbitral tribunal to consist of three arbitrators mentioning appointment of one each by the licensee and the licensor but omitted providing for appointment of a third arbitrator. But this did not prevent the court from applying the "officious bystander-principle", given that two arbitrators had been appointed by the parties. The missing line "two arbitrators appointed by the parties shall appoint the third arbitrator" was read into the arbitration clause.[10]"

- In *Chatterjee Petrochem Company* vs. *Haldia Petrochemicals Limited* 2014 (14) SCC 574 (2J) the Supreme Court held (on facts) that the arbitration clause in the agreement was valid, and not null and void and that the arbitration proceedings should continue.

- In *World Sport Group (Mauritius) Ltd.* vs. *MSM Satellite (Singapore) Pte. Ltd.*, 2014 (11) SCC 639 (at page 643) the Supreme Court of India held:

  > ". . . that an arbitration agreement does not become "inoperative or incapable of being performed" where allegations of fraud have to be inquired into, and the court cannot refuse to refer the parties to arbitration as provided in Section 45 of the 1996 Act on the ground that allegations of fraud have been made by the party which can only be inquired into by the court and not by the arbitrator. The court could decline to make a reference of a dispute covered by the arbitration agreement only if it came to the conclusion that the arbitration agreement was null and void, inoperative or incapable of being performed; not on the ground that allegations of fraud or misrepresentation had to be inquired into while deciding the disputes between the parties.[11]"

- In *Sasan Power Ltd.* vs. *North American Coal Corporation (India) (P) Ltd.*, 2016 (10) SCC 813 (2J) the Supreme Court of India emphasized that the scope of inquiry under Section 45 of the Act was confined only to the question whether the arbitration agreement was 'null and void or inoperative or incapable of being performed'. The legality and validity of the substantive contract could not be questioned under Section 45. The further contention that two Indian parties are not prevented from entering into an agreement for arbitration of their disputes to a seat outside India—though upheld by the judgment of the Division Bench of the High Court of Madhya Pradesh, (2016) 2 *Arbitration Law Reporter* 179 (MP)—was not commented on by the Supreme Court because the Supreme Court said it did not find anything to indicate that such a submission had been made before the High Court.[12] (As a matter of fact such a submission had been made before the High Court and the high court had pronounced its own view on it).

***

Section 46[13]—the next provision, ("When Foreign Awards are binding") reflects the provisions of Article III of the New York Convention which reads as follows:

> "Article III
> Each contracting state shall recognize arbitral awards as binding and enforce them in accordance with the rules of procedure of the territory where the award is relied upon, under the conditions laid down in the following articles. There shall not be imposed substantially more onerous conditions or higher fees or charges on the recognition or enforcement of arbitral awards to which this Convention applies than are imposed on the recognition or enforcement of domestic arbitral awards."

Leading commentaries (and cases) have described Article III as the source of the obligation of contracting states to recognise and enforce foreign arbitral awards[14]. In accordance with the wording of Article-III, courts of contracting states have applied the procedural rule of their respective national laws to the recognition and enforcement of arbitral awards, and not the laws of the courts where the arbitration took place or any other law[15].

The Supreme Court of India has said that the New York Convention was intended to allow contracting states to impose time-limits on the recognition and enforcement of foreign arbitral awards "if they so wished".[16]

***

Following upon Section 46, *Section* 47[17] ("Evidence") incorporates the essence of Article IV of the New York Convention. It reads as follows:

"Article IV

(1) To obtain the recognition and enforcement mentioned in the preceding article, the party applying for recognition and enforcement shall, at the time of the application, supply:

(a) The duly authenticated original award or a duly certified copy thereof;
(b) The original agreement referred to in article II or a duly certified copy thereof.

(2) If the said award or agreement is not made in an official language of the country in which the award

> is relied upon, the party applying for recognition and enforcement of the award shall produce a translation of these documents into such language. The translation shall be certified by an official or sworn translator or by a diplomatic or consular agent."

In *Yukos Oil Company* vs. *Dardana* (CA) [2002] EWCA Civ 543, the Court of Appeal (of England and Wales) in its judgment dated 18.4.2002, held that once a party has produced the duly authenticated award or a duly certified copy of it as well as the original arbitration agreement (or its duly certified copy), the party has a prima facie right to recognition and enforcement of the award.

Commentators have opined that an applicant satisfies the requirements of Article IV of the New York Convention even though a dissenting opinion (which exists) is not provided (unless the applicable rules provide otherwise) since a dissenting opinion does not form part of the award.[18]

***

Section 48 (1) and (2) (Conditions for enforcement of foreign awards), is one of the vital provisions in Part-II (as Section 34 is in Part-I).

Section 48 (1) and (2)[19] ("Conditions for Enforcement of Foreign Awards") is a reproduction of Article V of the New York Convention and is regarded as "the single most important provision of the Convention" (with Explanation I and Explanation II, separately added in India by Arbitration and Conciliation Amendment Act No. 3 of 2016)"[20]

The introductory sentence of Article V (1) provides that recognition and enforcement may only be refused "at the request of the party against whom [the award] is invoked, and if that party "furnishes proof" of the grounds listed in that Article." In accordance with this wording, courts in the contracting states have consistently recognised that the party opposing recognition and enforcement has the burden of first raising and then proving the grounds for non-enforcement under article V (1).[21]

Courts of the contracting states have held that the grounds for refusal under Article V(2) do not have to be pleaded by the party opposing recognition and enforcement.[22] While Article V(2) does not specifically allocate the burden of proof to either party, courts of the contracting states have considered that the party opposing recognition and enforcement has the ultimate burden of proving such grounds. Leading commentators on the Convention have expressed the same view.[23]

The list of grounds for refusal of recognition and enforcement as set out in Article V of the New York Convention—and reflected in the provisions contained in Sections 48(1) and (2)—are exhaustive. Article V expressly states that enforcement may be refused "only if" the requesting party furnishes evidence that one of the grounds set forth in Article V is fulfilled. The Convention does not envisage a refusal of enforcement based on other grounds.[24]

In his hypothetical draft convention on the international enforcement of arbitration agreements and awards, Prof. van den Berg, (General Editor of *ICCA Yearbook*) suggested that this should be stated even more explicitly by the re-wording of a new Article V(1): "Enforcement of an arbitral award shall not be refused on any ground other than the grounds expressly set forth in this article". But this comment is aspirational.

Section 48 states that enforcement of a foreign award *may* be refused at the request of the party against whom it is invoked only if that party furnishes to the court proof with regard to matters stated in Clauses (a) to (e) of Section 48(1), or in Clauses (a) or (b) of Section 48(2).

Since there were different judgments at different times by the Supreme Court of India on (foreign) awards, Explanations I and II were added to Section 48 of the Act (by Amending Act 3 of 2016) "for the removal of doubts": because it was felt that interpretation of the provisions of the 1996 Act by courts (including the Supreme Court of India in some cases) had resulted in delay in disposal of arbitration proceedings, and an increased interference of courts in arbitration matters tended to defeat the object of the Act.

Both sub-sections of Section 48 provide that enforcement "*may*" be refused, indicating clearly that the court has an ultimate discretion to reject the defence and to refuse enforcement of the foreign award. The court may find that the party opposing the enforcement is estopped from invoking any of the grounds mentioned in Section 48. It may also find that the "public policy" violation is not such as to prevent enforcement of the award. In proceedings for enforcement of a foreign award, the scope of enquiry before the court in which the award is sought to be enforced is limited to the conditions mentioned in Section 48. It is settled law that the Section does not enable a party to the said proceedings to impeach the foreign award on merits or for errors apparent on the face of the award.

In *Escorts Ltd.* vs. *Universal Tractor Holding LLC* reported in (2013) 10 SCC 717 the Supreme Court of India held, following a judgment of the English court, reported in *1991 (2) Lloyds Law Reports 625,* that the burden of proving that the award is not enforceable lies on the party that has raised the issue.[25]

Over the years, ever since the 1996 Act came into force, 'foreign awards' were filed for enforcement in the high courts of Bombay, Calcutta, Delhi, Madras and Madhya Pradesh. They are *forty-nine* in number, and except for *six* decisions (all of the High Court of Delhi), the foreign awards were ordered to be enforced. Particulars of these cases are mentioned below:

(i) Foreign awards that were held to be enforceable and were enforced under Section 48 in Part-II of 1996 Act by the high courts of Bombay[26], Calcutta[27], Delhi[28], Madras[29] and Madhya Pradesh[30] are mentioned in the respective endnotes. In eight of such cases Special Leave Petitions were filed in the Supreme Court of India but these were dismissed.

(ii) The foreign awards that were held to be not enforceable[31] under Section 48 in Part-II of the Act were of the High Court of Delhi.

Section 48(3)[32] reproduces Article VI of the New York Convention; which reads as follows:

> "Article VI
> If an application for the setting aside or suspension of the award has been made to a competent authority referred to in article V (1) (e), the authority before which the award is sought to be relied upon may, if it considers it proper, adjourn the decision on the enforcement of the award and may also, on the application of the party claiming enforcement of the award, order the other party to give suitable security."

Article VI of the Convention requires that if an application for setting aside or suspending an award has already been made before a competent authority, (In the absence of such an application) courts must refuse to adjourn the decision on the enforcement of the award.

In a case decided by the Supreme Court of New South Wales (in Australia) the court refused to grant an adjournment where the defendant had failed to establish that an application had been made before a competent authority (in Sweden) for the setting aside or suspension of the award.[33]

Commentaries on the New York Convention have noted (e.g. Wolff, ed [2012] at pages 438, 440) that pursuant to Article VI the competent authority (i.e. the courts) can decide on their own to adjourn enforcement proceedings. But the New York Convention 1958, does not provide that enforcement proceedings are to be automatically stayed when a setting aside application is brought. In appropriate circumstances, an award may be enforced despite a pending application to set it aside. The High Court of Justice in England and Wales (in its decision in *IPCO* vs. *Nigeria* of 27 April 2005[34]) has set out the appropriate circumstances:

(i) whether the application before the court in the country of origin is brought *bona fide* and not simply by way of delaying tactics;
(ii) whether the application before the court in the country of origin has at least a real (i.e. realistic) prospect of success; and
(iii) the extent of the delay occasioned by the potential adjournment, and the resulting prejudice.

The Supreme Court of British Columbia in the case of *Powerex Corp.* vs. *Alcan Inc*[35] has emphasized the "possibility–of–success-factor" in determining whether enforcement proceedings should (or should not) be adjourned. And the Court of Appeal in England in the case of *Soleh Boneh International Ltd* vs. *Government of the Republic of Uganda and National Housing Corporation* (judgment dated 12 March 1993)[36] has held that the most important factor for consideration is "*the strength of the argument*" (about the award being invalid").

***

Section 49: (Enforcement of Foreign Awards)[37]—there is no specific corresponding provision in the New York Convention, except perhaps Article III which provides that each contracting state shall recognise arbitral awards as binding and enforce them.

Section 49 however treats a foreign award as a *decree* of the court where the court is satisfied that the foreign award is *enforceable*—that is to say, when enforcement of the foreign award is not refused under Section 48 of the 1996 Act[38].

The following are decisions of the Supreme Court of India holding that foreign awards are to be treated as enforceable as "deemed" decrees of the court (Section 49):

- *Fuerst Day Lawson Ltd.* vs. *Jindal Exports Ltd.*, (2001) 6 SCC 356, where it was stated that the object of the Act being to minimise the supervisory role of the court and to give speedy justice, the stage of approaching the court for making the award a rule of court (as had been required in the Arbitration Act, 1940) has been dispensed with (in the 1996 Act); that separate proceedings do not have to be taken under the 1996 Act—first for deciding on enforceability of the award and make it a rule of the court, and thereafter to embark on execution proceedings—because "the very purpose of the 1996 Act in regard to speedy and effective execution of a foreign award will be defeated."
- *Fargo Freight Ltd.* vs. *Commodities Exchange Corpn.*, (2004) 7 SCC 203, where it was held (in an appeal against orders of the Delhi High Court) that an enforcement petition had necessarily to be between parties to the award, and that disputes regarding the

liability of third-persons could not be decided in such a proceeding.

- In *Centrotrade Minerals and Metal* vs. *Hindustan Copper Ltd*: 2017 (2) SCC 228 (3J), the Supreme Court of India held that a two-tier arbitration was permissible in law, and the arbitral award of the second tier (in London), would be enforceable in India as a 'foreign award'. An arbitration clause which provided that if either party was in disagreement with the result of an arbitration in India, either party had a right to appeal to a second arbitration in London, has been now held to be valid.

***

Section 50 (*Appealable Orders*)[39]—Obviously there is no corresponding provision in the New York Convention, 1958. On Section 50 of the Act, which deals with Appealable Orders, there are (at present) the following decisions of the Supreme Court of India:

- In *Sumitomo Corporation* vs. *CDC Financial Services, Mauritius & Ors.* reported in 2008 (4) SCC 91, the only question that was considered by the Supreme Court of India was whether an order passed by the Company Law Board (in a Company Petition under Sections 397-398 of the Companies Act, 1956 (now replaced by Sections 241 and 245 of the Companies Act, 2013) under Section 45 of the 1996 Act, refusing to refer parties to arbitration was liable to be challenged under Section 50 of the 1996 Act, or whether it could only be challenged as provided for in Section 10(1)(a) of the Companies Act, 1956. The High Court of Delhi held that the appeal under Section 50 of the 1996 Act was not maintainable—a decision affirmed by the Supreme Court of India.

- In *Shin-Etsu Chemical Company Limited (2) and Others* vs. *Vindhya Telelinks Limited and Others* reported in 2009 (14) SCC 16, the Supreme Court of India held that in the absence of a constitutional or statutory provision for an appeal as of right, an appellant could not contend that it had a right to appeal to the Supreme Court. An appeal by Special Leave to the Supreme Court under Article 136 cannot be considered an appeal as of right or as an appeal in pursuance of a right to appeal to the Supreme Court.
- In a later decision: *Kandla Export Corporation* vs. *OCI Corporation*: 2018 (14) SCC 715 (2J), the issue involved was whether an appeal, though not maintainable under Section 50 of the 1996 Act, was nonetheless maintainable under Section 13(1) of the commercial courts, Commercial Division And Commercial Appellate Division Of High Courts Act, 2015. The issue was answered in the negative. It was held that the 1996 Act was a self-contained code and exhaustive and carried with it the negative import that "only such acts as are mentioned in the Act are permissible to be done and acts or things not mentioned therein are not permissible to be done". It was also held that Section 50 was a self-contained provision on matters pertaining to arbitration and

was exhaustive. The court further held that since an appeal under Section 50 of the Arbitration and Conciliation Act 1996, was not maintainable, a Letters Patent Appeal from the decision of a single judge of the high court to that of a Division Bench of the high court was also not maintainable[40].

***

Section 51 (*Saving*)[41]—This is based on Article VII (1) of the New York Convention which reads:

> "1. The provisions of the present Convention shall not affect the validity of multilateral or bilateral agreements concerning the recognition and enforcement of arbitral awards entered into by the contracting states nor deprive any interested party of any right he may have to avail himself of an arbitral award in the manner and to the extent allowed by the law or the treaties of the country where such award is sought to be relied upon."

Most courts around the world have adopted the view that an interested party need not apply or request for recognition or enforcement on the basis of laws or treaties that are more favourable to enforcement. And it is said that a court will not be in breach of the New York Convention by applying more liberal rules on recognition and enforcement—even on its own motion. Article VII (1) also facilitates the recognition and enforcement or foreign arbitral awards by ensuring that contracting states will not be in breach of the New York Convention by enforcing arbitral awards pursuant to more favourable provisions found in their own domestic laws. In the year 2006, UNCITRAL adopted a "recommendation" regarding the interpretation *inter alia* of Article VII (1) of the New York Convention. It clarified that it should be applied to allow any interested party to avail itself of rights it may have under the laws or treaties of the country where an arbitration agreement is sought to be relied upon, to seek recognition of the validity of such an arbitration agreement.[42]

In India today, the Arbitration Act, 1940 having been repealed, it is under section 9 of the Code of Civil Procedure of 1908, that suits can be brought on a foreign award not covered by existing statute law. The relevant part of Section 9 reads:

> "9. Courts to try all civil suits unless barred: The courts shall (subject to the provisions herein contained) have jurisdiction to try all suits of a civil nature excepting suits of which their cognizance is either expressly or impliedly barred."

In all types of civil disputes, the civil courts had (and continue to have) *inherent* jurisdiction to entertain and try all suits of a civil nature—unless expressly or impliedly barred.

***

Section 52 (Chapter II not to apply)[43]

This section is based on Article VII (2) of the New York Convention which reads as follows:

> "2. The Geneva Protocol on Arbitration Clauses of 1923 and the Geneva Convention on the Execution of Foreign Arbitral Awards of 1927 shall cease to have effect between contracting states on their becoming bound and to the extent that they become bound by this Convention."

By a decision of the House of Lords in England (judgment dated 1 March 1984) in the case of in *Minister of Public Works of the Government of the State of Kuwait* vs. *Sir Fredric Snow & Partners* (reported in 1984 (1) Appeal Cases 426) it was held that the Geneva treaties ceased to apply to the recognition and enforcement of foreign arbitral awards in contracting states that had recognised and ratified the New York Convention.

Since the inception in 1976 of the *ICCA Yearbook*[44], it has reproduced extracts of decisions (of courts around the world) on the New York Convention, 1958. Extracts of decisions on the New York Convention of the Supreme Court of India, are published in the I*CCA Yearbooks* from the year 1976 onwards. Details are listed in the end notes.[45]

Geneva Convention Awards

The field of application of Chapter-II of Part-II (Geneva Convention Awards—Sections 53 to 60) is extremely limited, unlike Section 44 in Chapter-I of Part-II.

Section 53 applies only if the parties are subject to the jurisdiction of different parties to the Geneva Convention that had been notified by the Central Government. If an award made in the territory of a state which is not a party to the Geneva Convention, Chapter-II has no application. The states that had adhered to the Geneva Convention 1927 are substantially those that adhered to the Geneva Protocol of 1923, and the New York Convention 1958 expressly states in Article VII(2) that the New York Convention has replaced the 1923 Geneva Protocol and the 1927 Geneva Convention as between states that were party to both. As has been stated in a passage at page 269 (paragraph 269), in *Centrotrade Minerals and Metals Inc.* vs. *Hindustan Copper Ltd.* reported in 2006 (11) SCC 245—a case already cited:

> "Considering that the New York Convention has been ratified by 108 nations and less than five sovereign contracting states of the Geneva Convention have not become signatories to the New York Convention, *Chapter II of Part II of the 1996 Act already has minimal applicability and may soon have none at all, reducing that chapter to a surplusage.*"

The number of signatories (to the New York Convention) having already risen to 161 and hence any further comment on Part-II of Chapter-II is superfluous.

End Notes:

1. "44. Definition. In this chapter, unless the context otherwise requires, "foreign award" means an arbitral award on differences between persons arising out of legal relationships, whether contractual or not, considered as commercial under the law in force in India, made on or after the 11th day of October 1960:
   (a) in pursuance of an agreement in writing for arbitration to which the Convention set forth in the First Schedule applies, and
   (b) in one of such territories as the Central Government, being satisfied that reciprocal provisions have been made may, by notification in the official gazette, declare to be territories to which the said Convention applies."
2. The Supreme Court has held (under the Foreign Awards (Recognition and Enforcement) Act 1961) that while construing the expression "Commercial relationship" (in Section 44) aid can be taken from the Model Law (*R. M. Investment and Trading Co. Pvt. Ltd.* vs. *Boeing Co.*—AIR 1994 SC 1136 at pages 1139-1140).
3. Section 51 of the 1996 Act—"51. Saving.—Nothing in this Chapter shall prejudice any rights which any person would have had of enforcing in India of any award or of availing himself in India of any award if this Chapter had not been enacted."
4. Pursuant to the reciprocity provisions in the New York Convention Article I(3) and the general Article XIV: "A contracting state shall not be entitled to avail itself of the present Convention against other contracting state except to the extent that it is itself bound to apply the Convention".
5. "Section 45. Power of judicial authority to refer parties to arbitration. Notwithstanding anything contained in Part-I

or in the Code of Civil Procedure, 1908 (5 of 1908), a judicial authority, when seized of an action in a matter in respect of which the parties have made an agreement referred to in Section 44, shall, at the request of one of the parties or any person claiming through or under him, refer the parties to arbitration, unless it finds that the said agreement is null and void, inoperative or incapable of being performed." By the Arbitration and Conciliation (Amendment) Act 33 of 2019, for the words "unless it finds" the words "unless it prima facie finds" have been substituted.

6. https://www.arbitration-icca.org/media/0/12125884227980/New York Convention of 1958 overview.pdf
7. The decision of the High Court of Madras in the case of *Ramasamy Athappan* vs. *Secretariat of the Court of the ICC* is reported in 2009 (3) *Madras Law Journal* 84 (also available at http://indiankanoon.org/doc/218368).
8. The majority view appears to have been accepted by Parliament because by Amending Act 3 of 2016, Section 8 in Part-I (the counterpart of Section 45 in Part-II) was substituted for the originally enacted Section 8 by Amending Act 3 of 2016 with an entirely new provision. Under the substituted Section 8 (Power to refer parties to arbitration where there is an arbitration agreement), the finding that "no valid arbitration agreement exists" has to be prima facie ("the court shall refer the parties to arbitration "unless it finds that prima facie no valid arbitration agreement exist").
9. A similar view was taken by the full Bench of the High Court of Bombay in *J.S. Ocean LLC* vs. *M. V. Golden Progress* reported in 2007(2) Arb.L.R.104 (Bom.) (FB).

It has been held (in England) by the High Court of England of Wales that courts should conduct a cost analysis to determine whether the arbitration agreement is "null and void, 'inoperative' or incapable of being 'performed', and that it is better determined by the arbitral tribunal than by the courts: *A* vs. *B.* (2006) (High Court of Justice of England and Wales): EWHC (High Court of England and Wales) (Comm.), at page 2006.

10. A later decision of the Supreme Court of India has taken a similar view. In *Ameet Lalchand Shah and others* vs. *Rishab Enterprises* and other reported in AIR 2018 SC 3041, it was held that where parties were involved in a single commercial project (a solar plant), executed through several agreements with the main agreement containing an arbitration clause, the order of the Division Bench of the High Court of Delhi, declining to refer the dispute to arbitration, was unsustainable. All the four agreements in that case, and the parties thereto, were referred to arbitration. (But this was a decision rendered under Section 8 of the 1996 Act before its amendment. Section 8 of the 1996 Act, before its amendment by Act 3 of 2016, was a replica of Article 8 of the Model Law.
11. The decision has to be contrasted with an earlier decision of the Supreme Court of India in *A. Ayyaswamy* vs. *A. Paramsaivam & Ors*—2016 (10) SCC 386, where it was held that "serious allegations" of fraud were not arbitrable at all under the 1996 Act.
12. The High Court of Madhya Pradesh (Division Bench) had held that two Indian companies or Indian parties could arbitrate out of India, with seat of arbitration outside India, and said that in the case of *Atlas Export Industries* vs. *Kotak & Company* 1999 (3) Arb. L. R. 305 (SC), it had been settled that two Indians could agree to have a seat of arbitration outside India. The high court had also rejected the contention that two Indian companies were prevented from entering into a contract in derogation of Indian law

(a point on which the Supreme Court of India in 2016(10) SCC 813 expressed no opinion).

13. "Section 46. When foreign award binding: Any foreign award which would be enforceable under this chapter shall be treated as binding for all purposes on the persons as between whom it was made, and may accordingly be relied on by any of those persons by way of defence, set off or otherwise in any legal proceedings in India; and any references in this chapter to enforcing a foreign award shall be construed as including references to relying on an award."
14. Pieter Sanders: *ICCA's Guide to the Interpretation of the 1958 New York Convention: a Handbook for Judges*, 2011, at p. 691.
15. *ICCA Yearbook*, Vol. XXII, 1997 at p. 748.
16. *Yugraneft Corporation* vs. *Rexx Management Corporation* (29.05.2010) reported in 2010 (1) SCR 649 (Supreme Court of Canada).
17. Section 47. Evidence:
    (1) The party applying for the enforcement of a foreign award shall, at the time of the application, produce before the court:
        (a) the original award or a copy thereof, duly authenticated in the manner required by the law of the country in which it was made;
        (b) the original agreement for arbitration or a duly certified copy thereof;
        (c) such evidence as may be necessary to prove that the award is a foreign award.
    (2) If the award or agreement to be produced under sub-section (1) is in a foreign language, the party seeking to enforce the award shall produce a translation into English, certified as correct by a diplomatic or consular agent of the country to which that party

belongs or certified as correct in such other manner as may be sufficient according to the law in force in India.

Explanation—In this section, and in the sections following in this chapter, "Court" means the high court having original jurisdiction to decide the questions forming the subject-matter of the arbitral award if the same had been the subject-matter of a suit on its original civil jurisdiction and in other cases, in the high court having jurisdiction to hear appeals from decrees of courts subordinate to such High Court."

18. Emmanuel Galliard and John Savage: *Fouchard Galliard Goldman on International Commercial Arbitration*, Kluwer Law International, Netherlands, 1999, at p. 768, para 1404; Stavros Brekoulakis, Julian D. M. Lew and Loukas Mistelis, *The Evolution and Future of International Arbitration*; Wolters Kluwer, Netherland (2016) page 231 to 249.

19. Section 48. Conditions for enforcement of foreign awards:

    (1) Enforcement of a foreign award may be refused, at the request of the party against whom it is invoked, only if that party furnishes to the court, proof that:

    (a) the parties to the agreement referred to in Section 44 were, under the law applicable to them, under some incapacity, or the said agreement is not valid under the law to which the parties have subjected it or, failing any indication thereon, under the law of the country where the award was made; or

    (b) the party against whom the award is invoked was not given proper notice of the appointment of the arbitrator or of the arbitral proceedings or was otherwise unable to present his case; or

    (c) the award deals with a difference not contemplated by or not falling within the terms of the submission to arbitration, or it contains decisions on matters beyond the scope of the submission to arbitration; provided that, if the decisions on matters submitted to arbitration can be separated from those not so submitted, that part of the award which contains decisions on matters submitted to arbitration may be enforced; or

(d) the composition of the arbitral authority or the arbitral procedure was not in accordance with the agreement of the parties, or, failing such agreement, was not in accordance with the law of the country where the arbitration took place; or

(e) the award has not yet become binding on the parties, or, has been set aside or suspended by a competent authority of the country in which, or under the law of which, that award was made.

(2) Enforcement of an arbitral award may also be refused if the court finds that:

(a) the subject-matter of the difference is not capable of settlement by arbitration under the law of India; or

(b) the enforcement of the award would be contrary to the public policy of India.

Explanation 1—For the avoidance of any doubt it is clarified that an award is in conflict with the public policy of India only if:

(i) *the making of the award was induced or affected by fraud or corruption or was in violation of Section 75 (confidentiality) or Section 81 (non-advisability in evidence of consideration proceedings) or*

(ii) it is in contravention of the fundamental policy of Indian law, or

(iii) it is in conflict with the most basic notions of morality or justice.

Explanation 2—For the avoidance of doubt, the test as to whether there is a contravention with the fundamental policy of Indian law shall not entail a review on the merits of the dispute."

(Italicized portion added by Amending Act 3 of 2016)

20. The 246th Report of the Law Commission of India recommended the restriction of the scope of "public policy" in Section 48 (as well as Section 34). This was to bring the definition in line with the definition propounded by the Supreme Court in *Renusagar Power Plant Co. Ltd.* vs. *General Electric Co.* AIR 1994 SC 860 where the Supreme Court while construing the term "public policy" in Section 7(1)(b)(ii) of Foreign Awards (Recognition and Enforcement) Act, 1961 held that an award could be set aside if it was contrary to:

    (i) fundamental policy of Indian law;
    (ii) the interests of India; or
    (iii) justice or morality.

    The formulation proposed by the Law Commission was even stricter and did not include reference to "interests of India", which was vague and capable of "interpretational misuse", especially in the context of challenge to awards. Under the formulation of the Law Commission, an award could be set aside on public policy grounds only if it was opposed to the "fundamental policy of Indian law" or it was in conflict with "most basic notions of morality or justice".

    It has been also stated in the 246th Report of India's Law Commission, that the Supreme Court judgment in *ONGC* vs. *Western Geco. International Ltd.*—2014 (9) SCC 263, had construed the fundamental policy of India far too widely—which "no reasonable person would have arrived at"—and that a clarification was needed to be incorporated (as was later done by the explanations) added both in Section 34 and Section 48 of the 1996 Act)—to ensure that the "fundamental policy of Indian law" was narrowly construed. This has been explained (more recently) by the Supreme Court of India in its judgment dated 8 May 2019, in *Ssangyong Engineering & Construction Co. Ltd.* vs. *National Highway Authority of India* reported in 2019 (8) SCALE 41 at pages 60 to 64.

21. See, *Trans World Film Share Purchase Agreement* vs. *Film Polski Import and Export of Films*, Corte di Cassazione, February 1992, *ICCA Yearbook* Vol. XVIII, Pp. 433-436 (1993), Italy No. 123.
22. *Rosseel NV* vs. *Oriental Commercial Shipping*, High Court of Justice, England and Wales, 16 November 1990, *ICCA Yearbook*, Vol. XVI, 1991, Pp. 615-620.
23. Herbert Kronke, Patricia Nacimiento, Dirk Otto, Nicolo Christian Port (Eds.): *Recognition and Enforcement of Foreign Arbitral Awards: A Global Commentary on the New York Convention*, Kluwer Law International, Netherlands, Pp. 345, 348, 2010.
24. Albert Jan van den Berg: Hypothetical Draft Convention on the International Enforcement of Arbitration Agreements and Awards: Explanatory Note and Annexes, 50 Years of the New York Convention, ICCA Congress Series, No. 72, Kluwer Law International, Netherlands, 2009, Pp. 649-666.
25. In the case of *ONGC* vs. *Western Geco*: (2014) 9 SCC 263—a Bench of 3 judges of the Supreme Court dealt with the ground of "conflict with the public policy of India" following the decision in *ONGC* vs. *Saw Pipes*—2003 (5) SCC 705 and other prior decisions of the Supreme Court of India. But as already mentioned, this case is no longer good law since it was decided before the addition of the Explanation-1 and Explanation-2 by Amending Act No: 3 of 2016.

26. Bombay—1999(2) Arb.LR 383; 2000(1) Arb.LR 230; 2002(2) Arb.LR 560; 2006(3) Arb.L.R.510; 2008(1) Arb. LR 317; 2009(4) Arb.LR 298; 2012(2) Arb.LR 25; 2013(2) Arb.LR 270 (SLP dismissed 2015 (13) SCC 477); 2015(6) Arb.LR 172; 2016(2) Arb.LR 113; 2017(2) Arb.LR 290 (SLP dismissed 2016(9) SCC 526).
27. Calcutta—2005(2) Arb.LR 551 (Calcutta); 2012(3) Arb. LR 66; 2015(5) Arb.LR 370; 2017(4) Arb.LR 475; 2018(1) Arb.LR 441; 2019(1) Arb.LR 16 (SLP dismissed 2019(3) Scale 703).
28. Delhi—2004(3) Arb.LR 107 (Delhi); 2005(2) Arb.LR 6; 2007(4) Arb.LR 499; 2008(4) Arb.LR 326; 2008(4) Arb. LR 497; 2009(4) Arb.LR 272; 2009(Supp. 1) Arb.LR 307; 2011(1) Arb.LR 244; 2012 (Supp. 1) Arb.LR 143 (SLP dismissed 2014(2) SCC 433); 2012 (Supp. 2) Arb.LR 135; 2012(3) Arb.LR 434 (SLP dismissed 2013(10) SCC 717; 2012 (Supp. 1) Arb.LR 143 (SLP dismissed 2014(2) SCC 433; 2015(1) Arb.LR 113; 2016(6) Arb.LR 270; 2017(3) Arb.LR 21; 2017(4) Arb.LR 203; 2017(4) Arb. LR 228; 2018(1) Arb.LR 492 (SLP dismissed on 16.2.2018 unreported); 2018(4) Arb.LR 326; 2018(4) Arb.LR 415
29. Madras (Chennai) - 2005(3) Arb.LR 399 (Madras); 2015(1) Arb.LR 225; 2017(2) Arb.LR 321; 2017(3) Arb.LR 141; 2008(1) Arb.LR 344; 2019(2) Arb.L.R. 169
30. Madhya Pradesh - 2012 (Supp. 1) Arb.LR 94
31. (1) *Japan Travel Services* vs. *All Nippon Airways Company Ltd.* 2009(4) Arb.LR 432 (Section 48(1)(d));
    (2) Agritrade International PTD Ltd. vs. *NAFED* 2012(1) Arb.LR 405 (Section 48(2)(a)&(b));
    (3) Cinergy Corporation PTE Ltd. vs. *National Agricultural Co-operative Marketing Federation of India Ltd.* 2012 (Supp. 2) Arb.LR 418 (Section 7, 47(1)(b), 48(1)(a)&2(a));
    (4) Kalmart Systems (M) SDN BHD vs. *National*

Agricultural Co-operative Marketing Federation of India Ltd 2015(2) Arb.LR 479 (Section 48(1)(a));

(5) *Virgoz Oils and Fats Pvt. Ltd.* vs. *Nafed* 2017(1) Arb. LR 276 (Section 48(1) (a)& (c)). *Campos Brothers Farms* vs. *Matru Bhumi Supply Chain Pvt. Ltd.* 2019(3) Arb. L.R. 89 (Section 48(2)(b) read with Explanation 1(iii)).

32. "Section 48 (3). If an application for the setting aside or suspension of the award has been made to a competent authority referred to in clause (e) of sub-section (1) the court may, if it considers it proper, adjourn the decision on the enforcement of the award and may also, on the application of the party claiming enforcement of the award, order the other party to give suitable security."

33. In the case of *Lars Hallen, et al.* vs. *Sven-Olov Angledal, et al—ICCA Yearbook* 2004, Vol. XXIX. Pp. 520-532 (Australia No. 22).

34. [2005] EWHC 726 (Comm) [United Kingdom/ 27 April 2005/ England and Wales, High Court/ *IPCO* vs. *Nigeria (NNPC)*/ 2004 1031].

35. 2004 BCCA 504 [Canada / 04 October 2004 / Canada, Court of Appeal for British Columbia / *Powerex Corp.* vs. *Alcan Inc.*]

36. [1993] 2 Lloyd's Rep 208 [United Kingdom dated 12 March 1993].

37. 49. Enforcement of foreign awards—Where the court is satisfied that the foreign award is enforceable under this chapter, the award shall be deemed to be a decree of that court.

38. In an altogether different jurisdiction, a case from a US Federal Court has interpreted a non-Convention award as a "judgment" of a court. See *ICCA Yearbook* Vol. XXXI (2006) US No. 562, page-1352 to 1369 at page 1355:"The Convention 'governs judicial confirmation of arbitration

decisions that arise out of agreements between a US citizen and a citizen of a foreign nation that signed the Convention'. See *Publics Communication (France)* vs. *True North Communications Inc.* (USA), 206 F. 3d 725, 728 (7th Cir. 2000) (*Yearbook of Commercial Arbitration* Vol. XXV (2000) US 338, pages 1152 to 1157).

The New York Convention does not appear to bar the recognition of awards not falling under the Convention, including awards from non-signatory states such as Liechtenstein.

Among the reasons that actions to enforce foreign awards are brought outside the framework of the . . . Convention are that the country where the award was rendered is not a party to the Convention. . .: *Domke on Commercial Arbitration Sect.* 50:2 and n. 20 (2005); according to Restatement (Third) of Foreign Relations Law Sect. 487 (1987) ('Foreign arbitral awards not falling under the Convention are generally enforceable in the United States in the same manner as foreign judgments. . .whether or not they have been judicially confirmed in the state where made.")

39. "Section 50. Appealable orders:

(1) An appeal shall lie from the order refusing to (a) refer the parties to arbitration under section 45; (b) enforce a foreign award under section 48, to the court authorised by law to hear appeals from such order.

(2) No second appeal shall lie from an order passed in appeal under this Section, but nothing in this Section shall affect or take away any right to appeal to the Supreme Court." By the Arbitration and Conciliation (Amendment) Act 33_2019, in Section 50(1) for the words "An appeal" the words, "Notwithstanding anything contained in any other Law for the time being in force, an appeal" were substituted.

40. This decision is apparently inconsistent with the court's prior decision in *Arun Dev Upadhyaya* vs. *Integrated Sales Services Ltd.* – 2016 (9) SCC 524 (2J) though not referred to.
41. "**51.** *Saving*: Nothing in this chapter shall prejudice any rights which any person would have had of enforcing in India of any award or of availing himself in India of any award if this chapter had not been enacted.
42. Official records of the General Assembly, Sixty-First Session, Supplement No. 17(A/61/17), paras 177-181: available atwww.uncitral.org/pdf/english/texts/arbitration/NY-conv/A2E.pdf
43. "52. Chapter II not to apply: Chapter II of this Part shall not apply in relation to foreign awards to which this chapter applies."
44. *A complete list of all court decisions and awards published in the Yearbook since 1976 and a consolidated Index of cases are available online on the ICCA website www.arbitration-icca.org under the Publications button.*
45. Vol. I (1976) page 188 (decision of the Supreme Court of India); Vol. II (1977) pages 245-246 (decision of the High Court of Delhi); Vol. IV (1979) pages 270-274 (decision of the High Court of Kerala); Vol. VII (1982) pages 329-332 (decision of the Supreme Court of India); Vol. VIII (1983) pages 371-376 (decision of the High Court Appellate Branch of Bombay); Vol. IX (1984) pages 403-415 (decision of the High Court of Delhi); Vol. X (1985) pages 431-449 (Decision of the Supreme Court of India); Vol. XI (1986) pages 502-507 (decision of the High Court of Delhi); Vol. XIII (1988) pages 473-492, 493-496 and 497-503 (decisions of the Supreme Court of India, High Court of Delhi and High Court of Calcutta); Vol. XIV (1989) pages 644-647, 648-662, 663-672 (decisions of the High Court of Bombay, High Court of Gujarat, and the Supreme Court of India);

Vol. XV (1990) pages 465-492 (decision of the High Court of Bombay); Vol. XVI (1991) pages 553-573; 574-584 (decisions of the High Court of Bombay and High Court of Delhi); Vol. XVIII (1993) pages 403-414 (decision of the Supreme Court of India); Vol. XX (1995) pages 681-738 (decision of the Supreme Court of India); Vol. XXI (1996) pages 552-556; 557-570 (decisions of the Supreme Court of India); Vol. XXII (1997) Pages 710-714 (decision of the Supreme Court of India); Vol. XXIII (1998) pages 688-712, 713-718 (decisions of the High Court of Delhi and Court of Appeal); Vol. XXIVa (1999) pages 678-687, 688-695 (decisions of the Supreme Court of India and High Court of Delhi); Vol. XXV (2000) pages 721-733 and 734-738 (decisions of Supreme Court of India); Vol. XXVI (2001) pages 780-782, 783-787 and 788-806 (decisions of the Bombay and Delhi High Court); Vol. XXVII (2002) pages 455-465, 466-477, 478-481 and 482-491 (decisions of the Bombay High Court and Supreme Court of India); Vol. XXVIII (2003) pages 790-809 (decision of the High Court of Gujarat); Vol. XXX (2005) pages 577-590 (decision of the High Court of Andhra Pradesh); Vol. XXXI (2006) pages 747-785 (decision of the Supreme Court of India); Vol. XXXIV (2009) pages 611-620 and 621-631 (decisions of the Supreme Court of India); Vol. XXXV (2010) pages 398-400 and 401-403 (decisions of the High Court of Gujarat and High Court of Delhi); Vol. XXXVI (2011) pages 293-295 (decision of the High Court of Delhi); Vol. XXXVII (2012) pages 242-243 and 244-249 (decisions of the High Court of Calcutta and of the Supreme Court of India); Vol. XXXVIII (2013) pages 392-396 and 397-400 (decisions of the Supreme Court of India); Vol. XXXIX (2014) pages 406-407 and 408-412 (decisions of the Supreme Court of India); Vol. XLII (2017) pages 402-406, 407-411 and 412-414 (decisions of the Supreme Court of

India and High Court of Delhi); Vol. XLIII (2018) pages 455-458, 459-465 and 466-470 (decisions of the High Court of Delhi and High Court of Judicature, Rajasthan). Cases that will probably be published in the *ICCA Yearbook Commercial Arbitration* 2019 Vol.-XLIV are: (i) India No. 2019-1, *P.E.C. Ltd.* vs. *Austbulk Shipping SDN BHD*, Supreme Court of India, Civil Appeal No: 4834 of 2007, 14 November 2018 (/document/KLI-KA-ICCA-YB-XLIV-307n); (ii) India No. 2019-2, *Kandla Export Corporation et al.* vs. *OCI Corporation et al.*, Supreme Court, Civil Appeal No; 1661-1663 of 2018, 7 February 2018 (/document/KLI-KA-ICCA-YB-XLIV-405-n); and (iii) India No. 2019-3, *Shriram EPC Limited* vs. *Rioglass Solar SA*, Supreme Court, Civil Appeal No. 9515 of 2018, 13 September 2018 (/document/KLI-ICCA-YB-XLIV-406-n)"

7

The Role of the Conciliator

Independent, Impartial, Considerate

Part-III: CONCILIATION

In Part-III, Sections 61 to 81 correspond to the UNCITRAL Conciliation Rules 1980[1]. The only provision that is not a reproduction of the 1980 Rules is Section 66 which provides:

> "*Conciliator not bound by certain amendments*: The conciliator is not bound by the Code of Civil Procedure, 1908 (5 of 1908) or the Indian Evidence Act, 1872."

On the role of the Conciliator (Section 67), in a judgment of the Supreme Court of India[2] it has been said: (Whilst contrasting the provisions in the Legal Services Authorities Act, 1987 with the provisions relating to Conciliation in Part-III of the 1996 Act):

> "22. The term "conciliation" is not defined under the (1987) Act. It should, therefore, be considered from the perspective of the Arbitration and Conciliation Act, 1996. In order to understand what Parliament meant by "Conciliation", we have necessarily to refer to the functions of a "Conciliator" as visualised by Part III of the 1996 Act. Section 67 describes the role of a conciliator:
>
> Sub-section (1) states that he shall assist parties in an independent and impartial manner.
>
> Sub-section (2) states that he shall be guided by principles of objectivity, fairness and justice, giving

consideration, among other things, to the rights and obligations of the parties, the usages of the trade concerned and the circumstances surrounding the dispute, including any previous business practices between the parties.

Sub-section (3) states that he shall take into account «the circumstances of the case, the wishes the parties may express, including a request for oral statements».

Sub-section (4) is important and permits the "conciliator" to make proposals for a settlement. This section is based on Article 7 of UNICTRAL Conciliation Rules.

23. Section 73, which is important, states that the conciliator can formulate terms of a possible settlement if he feels that there exist elements of settlement. He is also entitled to "reformulate the terms" after receiving the observations of the parties. The above provisions in the 1996 Act, make it clear that the "Conciliator" under the said Act, apart from assisting the parties to arrive at a settlement, is also permitted to make "proposals for a settlement" and "formulate the terms of a possible settlement" or "reformulate the terms". This is indeed the UNCITRAL concept."

In the same case, the Supreme Court of India then contrasted the role of "conciliator" in Part-III of the 1996 Act, with that of a conciliator under Chapter-VIA of the Legal Services Authorities Act 1987, and observed:

"24. Section 89 of the Code of Civil Procedure inter alia was enacted to promote resolution of disputes through mutual settlement. Chapter VI-A of the Act seeks to achieve a different purpose. It not only speaks of conciliation qua conciliation but conciliation qua determination. Jurisdiction of the Permanent Lok Adalat, although limited is of wide amplitude. The two Provisos appended to Section 22-C (1) of the Act curtail the jurisdiction of the Permanent Lok Adalat which are as under:

- Provided that the Permanent Lok Adalat shall not have jurisdiction in respect of any matter relating to an offence not compoundable under any law.
- Provided further that the Permanent Lok Adalat shall also not have jurisdiction in the matter where the value of the property in dispute exceeds ten lakh rupees."

Whilst assimilating the Role of a Conciliator under Part-III of the 1996 Act, on his assuming the role of an arbitrator, (where no settlement is possible in conciliation), the Supreme Court distinguished the role of the Permanent Lok Adalat under the Legal Services Authorities Act, 1987. In the latter case the words quoted in the Proviso to Section 22(C)(1) of the Legal Services Authorities Act, 1987, were construed broadly and it was held that the determination before the Permanent Lok Adalat (in that particular case) necessarily involved a question as to whether or not an offence "which is non-compoundable in nature has indeed been committed", it was held that the case fell outside the jurisdiction of the Permanent Lok Adalat and, therefore, the order of the High Court of Jharkhand upholding the validity of the order was set aside.

***

The UNCITRAL Model Law on International Commercial Conciliation 2002, which came later—after the UNCITRAL Conciliation Rules, 1980—has not yet been adopted by India. It contains the following 14 Articles:

Article 1.	Scope of application and definitions
Article 2.	Interpretation
Article 3.	Variation by agreement
Article 4.	Commencement of conciliation proceedings
Article 5.	Number and appointment of conciliators
Article 6.	Conduct of conciliation
Article 7.	Communication between conciliator and parties
Article 8.	Disclosure of information
Article 9.	Confidentiality
Article 10.	Admissibility of evidence in other proceedings
Article 11.	Termination of conciliation proceedings
Article 12.	Conciliator acting as arbitrator
Article 13.	Resort to arbitral or judicial proceedings
Article 14.	Enforceability of settlement agreement

Text of this Model Law is available on the website of UNCITRAL.

This Model Law of International Commercial Conciliation 2002 is in two Parts—Part-I which contains the above 14 Articles, and Part-II which is a *Guide* to the Enactment and Use of the Law.

The *Guide* is drawn from the *travaux préparatoires* of the UNCITRAL Model Law on International Commercial Conciliation. It explains why the provisions in the Model Law have been included as essential basic features of a statutory device designed to achieve the objectives of the Model Law. When it drafted the model law, the Commission had assumed that the explanatory material would accompany the text of the Model Law. However, it did not. Additionally, some issues, not settled in the Model Law, have been addressed in the *Guide*, which is designed to provide an additional source of inspiration to states enacting the Model Law. It might also assist states in considering which provisions of the Model Law, if any, might have to be varied to accommodate particular national circumstances.

This *Guide* has been prepared by the secretariat pursuant to a request made by UNCITRAL. It reflects the deliberations and decisions of the Commission during the session at which the Model Law was adopted, and the considerations of UNCITRAL's Working Group-II (on Arbitration and Conciliation) that conducted the preparatory work.

***

The UNCITRAL Model Law on International Commercial Conciliation Guide to Enactment and Use of the UNCITRAL Model Law on International Commercial Conciliation

(2002) is a UN Publication which can be downloaded from https://www.uncitral.org/pdf/english/texts/arbitration/ml-conc/03-90953_Ebook.pdf.[3]

The UNCITRAL Model Law on International Commercial Conciliation (2002) has now been further amended by the UNCITRAL Model Law on International Commercial Mediation and International Settlement Agreements (2018), resulting from Mediation 2018—which has come into force from 7 August 2019, (now known as The Singapore Convention) after it was signed by 46 countries.

***

Part-IV—Supplementary Provisions

(Section 82 (Power of High Court to make rules); Section 83 (Removal of difficulties); Section 84 (Power to make rules); Section 85 and 86[4] (Repeal and saving)—along with Eight Schedules viz.

- the First Schedule (is a verbatim copy of the entire text of the New York Convention, 1958.
- the Second Schedule (contains the text of the Geneva Protocol on Arbitration Clauses 1923.
- the Third Schedule (contains the text of the Geneva Convention on the Execution of Foreign Arbitral Awards 1927.
- the Fourth Schedule (enables high courts to fix fees of arbitral tribunals with a suggested model fee).

- the Fifth Schedule (specifies grounds giving rise to justifiable doubts as to the independence or impartibility of arbitrators).
- the Sixth Schedule (circumstances likely to affect the independence or impartibility or arbitrators); (the fifth and sixth schedules had been added by Amendment Act 3 of 2016).
- the Seventh Schedule (mentions categories of persons ineligible to be appointed Arbitrators).
- the Eighth Schedule (prescribes qualifications and experience of arbitrators)[5] has been added by the Amending Act No. 33 of 2019 in August 2019).

By amending Act 33 of 2019 (enacted in August 2019) a new Section 87 has been introduced in the 1996 Act reading as follows:

> "Unless the parties otherwise agree, the amendments made to this Act by the Arbitration and Conciliation (Amendment) Act, 2015 shall
>
> (a) not apply to–
>
> (i) arbitral proceedings commenced before the commencement of the Arbitration and Conciliation (Amendment) Act, 2015;
> (ii) court proceedings arising out of or in relation to such arbitral proceedings, irrespective of whether such court proceedings are commenced prior to or after the commencement of the Arbitration and Conciliation (Amendment) Act, 2015;

(b) apply only to arbitral proceedings commenced on or after the commencement of the Arbitration and Conciliation (Amendment) Act, 2015 and to court proceedings arising out of or in relation to such arbitral proceedings."

This Section has been trenchantly criticised in the case of B*CCI vs. Kochi Cricket Pvt Ltd.* reported in 2018 (6) SCC 287 by the Supreme Court of India:

> "Section 87 has purported to delete Section 26[6] of the Amendment Act 2015 (Act 3 of 2015) *which has resulted in the slowing down of reforms in Arbitration Law.*"

The Court has also stated that:

> The immediate effect of the proposed Section 87 would be to put all the important amendments made by the Amending Act of 2015 (Act 3 of 2016) on a back burner".

Conclusion:

It is submitted that in the light of the observations by the Supreme Court of India in 2018 (6) SCC 287, Section 87 should be deleted so that Section 26 of the Amendment Act of 2015—Act 3 of 2016—(in furtherance of comprehensive arbitral reforms) gets restored.

> **Note**: After the first edition of this volume (*The Arbitration Series Vol.-1*), Section 87, has been struck

down as "manifestly arbitrary" under Article 14 of the Constitution of India: by a Bench of three judges of the Supreme Court of India (judgment dated 27 November 2019 reported in 2019 (16) Scale 823 (this judgment in the case of *Hindustan Construction Co. Ltd.* vs. *Union of India*—is also available on: SCC Online 2019 SC 1520).

End Notes:

1. Available at: https://www.uncitral.org/pdf/english/texts/arbitration/conc-rules/conc-rules-e.pdf

   The Judicial Academy of Jharkhand has compiled "Case Laws on Mediation" containing 11 judgments of the Supreme Court of India reported in: 2003(1) SCC 49; 2005(6) SCC 34; 2005(6) SCC 478; 2008(2) SCC 660; 2008(7) SCC 454; 2009(2) SCC 198 & 511; 2010(8) SCC 24; 2010(15) SCC 286; 2011(1) SCC 466; and 2011(15) SCC 464.
2. Judgment dated 13 May 2008, in *United India Insurance Co., Ltd.,* vs. *Ajay Sinha & Anr*: reported in 2008 (7) SCC 454.
3. The UNCITRAL Model Law of Conciliation 2002 has not been adopted by India (See its criticism in (2004) Vol.21(1) Journal of International Arbitration, page 1 at page 7).
4. Section 85 repeals the Arbitration (Protocol and Convention) Act, 1937, the Arbitration Act, 1940 and the Foreign Awards (Recognition and Enforcement) Act, 1961, but saves the provisions of the said enactments that applied in relation to artibral proceedings which commenced before the Arbitration and Conciliation Act, 1996, came into force;

Section 86 repeals the Arbitration and Conciliation (Third) Ordinance, 1996, which was replaced by the Act No.26 of 1996, but saved any Rule, order or notification or scheme made or anything done or any action taken in pursuance of the said Ordinance.

5. The Eighth Schedule has been added by Section 43J of the Arbitration and Conciliation Amendment Act 33 of 2019.
6. "26. Nothing contained in this Act shall apply to the arbitral proceedings commenced, in accordance with the provisions of Section 21 of the principal Act, before the commencement of this Act unless the parties otherwise agreed but this Act shall apply in relation to arbitral proceedings commenced on or after the date of commencement of this Act."

Selected Bibliography

1. "*A Guide to UNCITRAL Model Law on International Commercial Arbitration: Legislative History and Commentary*" by Howard Holtzmann and Joseph Neuhas published by Kluwer Law and Taxation, Netherlands (1989). It contains an article-by-article commentary – precise and coherent – on the UNCITRAL Model Law, 1985, and though first published in 1989 is still topical and instructive. It also contains proceedings of the Working Group on each of the Articles of the Model Law. It is a must-read for arbitrators and practitioners in arbitration who want to know the whys-and-wherefores of the UNCITRAL Model Law, 1985.
2. In a later publication, also by Howard Holtzman and Joseph Neuhaus (but along with Edda Kristjansdottir and Thomas W. Walsh), titled "*A Guide to the 2006 Amendments to the UNCITRAL Model Law on International Commercial Arbitration: Legislative History and Commentary*" (Published by Wolters Kluwer, Kluwer Law International, Netherland, 2015): there is an up-date of item 1 above.
3. *UNCITRAL Model Law on International Commercial Arbitration* (*with amendments adopted in 2006*)—United Nations, Vienna, 2008 – a UN publication is available and can be downloaded from website: https://www.uncitral.org/pdf/english/ texts/arbitration/ml-arb/07-86998_Ebook.pdf
4. Cases decided by courts in the states/territories that have adopted the UNCITRAL Model Law are regularly reported in CLOUT—*Case Law on UNCITRAL Texts: A legal database of worldwide court decisions and arbitral awards on UNCITRAL – they* can be down-loaded from:
https://www.uncitral.org/uncitral/en/case_law.html
5. "*Model Law Decisions*" Case-law from 1985 to 2001 containing extracts of cases on the Model Law decided by

Courts around the world are contained in a book authored by a trio of international arbitrators: Henri C. Alvarez, Neil Kaplan and David W. Rivkin, published by Kluwer Law International, The Hague. It includes a case-synopsis from the Supreme Court of British Columbia, from the Supreme Court of Canada, from the High Court of Hong Kong, from the High Court of Singapore, and from courts in other countries as well.

6. "*International Arbitration*" by Martin Hunter and Alan Redfern published by Oxford University Press, 6th Edition (2015) (earlier edition – 3rd Edition) was under the title "*Law and Practice of International Commercial Arbitration*" (2004).
7. "*Comparative International Commercial Arbitration*", by Julian DM Lew, Lucas A. Mistelis and Stefan M. Kroll published by Kluwer Law International: The Hague/London/New York (2003).
8. "*Principles and Practice of International Commercial Arbitration*", by Margaret Moses published by Cambridge University Press: Cambridge, (2008).
9. "*International Commercial Arbitration and Mediation in UNCITRAL Model Law Jurisdictions' by* Dr Peter Binder, published by Wolters Kluwer, Netherlands (4th Edition, 2019). *It gives various references and citations of court decisions around the world reported in CLOUT (Case Law on UNCITRAL Text) available at: (http://www.uncitral.org/clout)) for each and every Article (Articles 1 to 36) of the UNCITRAL Model Law*—(in respect of which the roughly corresponding provisions of India's 1996 Act (as amended in 2015 and 2019) are Sections 2 to 36).
10. "*The Evolution and Future of International Arbitration*", by Brekoulakis Stavros, Julian D.M. Lew and Loukas Mistelis, published by Wolters Kluwer (2016).

11. *"International Commercial Arbitration"*, by Fouchard Philippe, Goldman Berthold: published by Kluwer Law International: The Hague, (1999).
12. *"International Commercial Arbitration"* by Jay E. Grenig published by Thomson Reuters/South Asian Edition: New Delhi, (2014).
13. *"The Osler Guide to Commercial Arbitration in Canada,"*: a practical introduction to domestic and international commercial arbitration by Barin Babak, Andrew D. Little, Randy Pepper, published by Kluwer Law International, 1st Edition (2006).
14. "*A Guide to UNCITRAL: Basic facts about the United Nations Commission on International Trade Law*": a UN Publication (2013)

    It can be downloaded from:

    https://www.uncitral.org/pdf/english/texts/ general/12-57491-Guide-to-UNCITRAL-e.pdf

    Its table of contents include:

    1. Origin, mandate and membership of UNCITRAL;
    2. General Information on UNCITRAL;
    3. Organisation and methods of work;
    4. Work of UNCITRAL.
15. "*The Law Relating to International Commercial Disputes*", LLP London, 2nd Edition (1998) by Jonathan Hill
16. "*Guide on the Convention on the Recognition and Enforcement of Foreign Arbitral Awards—New York 1958,*" by Emmanuel Gaillard and George A. Bermann (Eds.): published by (the UNCITRAL Secretariat) BRILL NIJHOFF, Leiden, Boston, USA, (2017). *(This book also contains references to cases on each and every Article of the New York Convention).*
17. In 2012, Shearman and Sterling and the Columbia Law School launched, in cooperation with UNCITRAL (a website on: the New York Convention 1958.org). It is

the product of a coordinated effort to create an interactive online platform that makes information gathered during the preparation of the Guide on the New York Convention publicly available.

The new version of the website, launched on 8th July 2016, complements the Guide through its sophisticated global legal database. *Today, this website goes beyond its initial objective and endeavours to collect and share new data, published worldwide, on the application and interpretation of the New York Convention.*

18. "*The 1958 New York Convention in Action" by* Marike Paulsson published by Kluwer Law International, Netherland, (2016).
19. Dr. Reinmar Wolff (Editor): "*New York Convention on the Recognition and Enforcement of Foreign Arbitral Awards—Commentary*", published by Verlag C. H. BECK (Nomos), Munich, Germany, (2012).
20. *"New Trends in the Development of International Commercial Arbitration and the Role of Arbitral and other Institutions International Council for Commercial Arbitration Congress"*: by Pieter Sanders: London, (1983)
21. *"International Arbitration Law and Practice"*; by Rubino – Sammartano M published by Kluwer Law International 2nd Edition (*2001*) Hague.
22. *"UNCITRAL ARBITRATION Model Law in Canada*', by Robert Paterson and Bonita Thompson published by Carswell Legal Publications, Canada (1987).
23. *"Handbook of ICC Arbitration Commentary, Precedents, Materials"* by Michael Buhler and Thomas H Webster published by Sweet and Maxwell, London 2nd Edition: (2010).
24. "*Handbook of UNCITRAL Arbitration – Commentary, Precedents & Models for UNCITRAL"* – based Arbitration Rules, (2nd Edition) by Thomas H. Webster published by Sweet & Maxwell, UK, (2014).

Acknowledgements

I am immensely indebted to my colleague Subhash Sharma for his most useful inputs. But for him this volume *would* not have been possible.

I must also express sincere thanks to my good friend Sumeet Kachwaha, Senior Partner of Kachwaha & Partners Law Offices, Delhi, for his help, and particularly for the extremely useful services of his very bright and energetic assistant Aayush Marwah, who has been on call on innumerable occasions and has always responded positively.

My grateful thanks to my entire staff—in particular my Secretary Vinod Anand—along with my additional secretaries Narender Kumar, Vinod Kumar and Lakhvinder for undertaking the laborious task of typing and re-typing drafts hundreds of times.

PRAISE FOR

BEFORE MEMORY FADES ...an autobiograpy

Whoever has heard Fali S. Nariman … never ceased to be impressed by his eloquence, command of the language, and a flair for the apt phrase. All these attributes are at their height in his autobiography *Before Memory Fades* that is lucid, concise, witty and absorbing; … not just a good read, it is also a delightful one. For those who have anything to do with law—its formulation, enforcement or practice—it should be compulsory reading.

—*India Today*

Billed as "An Autobiography", Nariman's book is less a continuous narrative than a collection of reminiscences, anecdotes and reflections on the events and people that have filled his very full life—recounted with that ineffable charm, gentle persuasiveness and quiet humour that so charaterise the man.… There is much else—on the Emergency and its judges, on fellow-lawyers and court anecdotes, a brilliant chapter on river water disputes and engaging reflections on his tenure as a nominated member of the Rajya Sabha. I commend this easy and profitable read.

—*Outlook*

Over the decades Fali S. Nariman has attained the status of a pre-eminent advocate whose views are not only heard but also respected. This autobiography is informative, educative and thought-provoking.… It isn't the content alone that makes this book an endearing read. This autobiography is suffused with a rare warmth and modesty, a spirit of liberalism reflected in the willingness to seriously address rival points of view, and a scholarship that is worn very lightly.… All in all, a compassionate work written by someone who comes across as a compassionate man.

—*The Hindu*

Fali Nariman's autobiography … is a joy to read. No doubt the author starts at the beginning but it's not his life story he relates so much as an honest account of the important events that stood out in his life.… It is exceptional for two other reasons. … First, it deftly avoids the pitfalls most memoirs inevitably hurtle towards and, second, it discovers the real secret of a delightful read.… He's not just the raconteur but the man in the middle too. An autobiography that makes you think. The author makes you engage with the book rather than simply read it.

—*Hindustan Times*

The book is brilliantly planned and beautifully designed. The 18 chapters, laced with quotations, anecdotes and series of vignettes … provide a glimpse of his jurisprudential wisdom.… It is a must not only for judges, advocates, students of law and political science, but also for editors, people's representatives, administrators, academics and all those who believe in the sanctity of constitutional values, the majesty of law and, above all, independence of the judiciary.

—*The Tribune*

What makes his autobiography very readable is the all-pervading sense of modesty and touches of humour.

—Khushwant Singh

Fali S. Nariman, the legal luminary, lifts the dark veil from the facts long shielded from public view in his autobiography *Before Memory Fades.* Nariman serves us shining examples of the exceptions, both of the bench and the bar.

—*Business Standard*